MEMORIES
of
HEAVEN

Other Hay House Products
by DR. WAYNE W. DYER

BOOKS

Being in Balance
Change Your Thoughts—Change Your Life
Co-creating at Its Best (with Esther Hicks)
Don't Die with Your Music Still in You (with Serena Dyer)
Everyday Wisdom
Everyday Wisdom for Success
Excuses Begone!
Getting in the Gap (book-with-audio)
Good-bye, Bumps! (children's book with Saje Dyer)
I Am (children's book with Kristina Tracy)
I Can See Clearly Now
Incredible You! (children's book with Kristina Tracy)
Inspiration
The Invisible Force
It's Not What You've Got! (children's book with Kristina Tracy)
Living the Wisdom of the Tao
My Greatest Teacher (with Lynn Lauber)
No Excuses! (children's book with Kristina Tracy)
The Power of Intention
The Power of Intention gift edition
A Promise Is a Promise
The Shift
Staying on the Path
10 Secrets for Success and Inner Peace
Unstoppable Me! (children's book with Kristina Tracy)
Your Ultimate Calling
Wishes Fulfilled

AUDIO/CD PROGRAMS

Advancing Your Spirit (with Marianne Williamson)
Applying the 10 Secrets for Success and Inner Peace
The Caroline Myss & Wayne Dyer Seminar
Change Your Thoughts—Change Your Life (unabridged audio book)
Change Your Thoughts Meditation
Co-creating at Its Best (unabridged audio book)
Divine Love
Dr. Wayne W. Dyer Unplugged (interviews with Lisa Garr)
Everyday Wisdom (audio book)
Excuses Begone! (available as an audio book and a lecture)
How to Get What You Really, Really, Really, Really Want
I AM Wishes Fulfilled Meditation (with James Twyman)
I Can See Clearly Now (unabridged audio book)

The Importance of Being Extraordinary (with Eckhart Tolle)
Inspiration (abridged 4-CD set)
Inspirational Thoughts
Making the Shift (6-CD set)
Making Your Thoughts Work for You (with Byron Katie)
Meditations for Manifesting
101 Ways to Transform Your Life (audio book)
The Power of Intention (abridged 4-CD set)
A Promise Is a Promise (audio book)
Secrets of Manifesting
The Secrets of the Power of Intention (6-CD set)
10 Secrets for Success and Inner Peace
There Is a Spiritual Solution to Every Problem
The Wayne Dyer Audio Collection/CD Collection
Wishes Fulfilled (unabridged audio book)

DVDs

Change Your Thoughts—Change Your Life
Co-creating at Its Best (with Esther Hicks)
Excuses Begone!
Experiencing the Miraculous
I Can See Clearly Now
The Importance of Being Extraordinary (with Eckhart Tolle)
Inspiration
Modern Wisdom from the Ancient World
My Greatest Teacher (a film with bonus material featuring Wayne)
The Power of Intention
The Shift, the movie (available as a 1-DVD program and an expanded
2-DVD set)
10 Secrets for Success and Inner Peace
There's a Spiritual Solution to Every Problem
Wishes Fulfilled

MISCELLANEOUS

The Essential Wayne Dyer Collection (comprising *The Power of Intention*,
Inspiration, and *Excuses Begone!* in a single volume)
Everyday Wisdom 2016 Calendar
Inner Peace Cards
The Power of Intention Cards
The Shift Box Set (includes *The Shift* DVD and *The Shift* tradepaper book)
10 Secrets for Success and Inner Peace Cards
10 Secrets for Success and Inner Peace gift products: *Notecards, Candle,*
and *Journal*

All of the above are available at your local bookstore, or may be ordered
by visiting: Hay House USA: www.hayhouse.com; Hay House Australia:
www.hayhouse.com.au; Hay House UK: www.hayhouse.co.uk; Hay House
South Africa: www.hayhouse.co.za; Hay House India: www.hayhouse.co.in

MEMORIES OF HEAVEN

CHILDREN'S ASTOUNDING RECOLLECTIONS OF THE TIME BEFORE THEY CAME TO EARTH

DR. WAYNE W. DYER
AND
DEE GARNES

HAY HOUSE, INC.
Carlsbad, California • New York City
London • Sydney • Johannesburg
Vancouver • Hong Kong • New Delhi

Published and distributed in the United States by: Hay House, Inc.: www.hayhouse
.com® • *Published and distributed in Australia by:* Hay House Australia Pty. Ltd.: www
.hayhouse.com.au • *Published and distributed in the United Kingdom by:* Hay House
UK, Ltd.: www.hayhouse.co.uk • *Published and distributed in the Republic of South
Africa by:* Hay House SA (Pty), Ltd.: www.hayhouse.co.za • *Distributed in Canada by:*
Raincoast Books: www.raincoast.com • *Published in India by:* Hay House Publishers
India: www.hayhouse.co.in

Cover design: Amy Rose Grigoriou • *Interior design:* Rhett Nacson

Editor's note: All stories in this book have been edited for length and clarity. An asterisk (*) next to a contributor's name indicates that his or her location was not provided.

Library of Congress Cataloging-in-Publication Data

Dyer, Wayne W.
  Memories of heaven : children's astounding recollections of the time before they came to earth / Dr. Wayne W. Dyer and Dee Garnes. -- 1st edition.
    pages cm
  ISBN 978-1-4019-4852-8 (hardcover : alk. paper) 1. Reincarnation--Case studies. 2. Children--Psychic ability--Case studies. 3. Heaven. 4. Memory in children--Miscellanea. I. Title.
  BL515.D94 2015
  133.901'35--dc23
                            2015024203

Hardcover ISBN: 978-1-4019-4852-8

11 10 9 8 7 6 5 4 3 2
1st edition, October 2015

Printed in the United States of America

To Sailor, our newest arrival.
— Wayne

To my husband, Trey; and our children,
Marcus and Shiloh.
— Dee

CONTENTS

INTRODUCTION

BY DR. WAYNE W. DYER

I have enjoyed a lifetime love affair with children, particularly newborns, infants, and toddlers. If a baby is in the room, it's almost as if there is a magnetic connection that draws my attention and I must make contact. Being the father of eight children, I have spent countless hours simply gazing into the eyes of a brand-new arrival into our family. In these private moments, I often send silent inquisitive messages asking them to tell me about God and what the formless spiritual world is like.

I have passed many, many hours of my life lying on the floor making direct contact with our new arrivals. I've long been fascinated by the fact that children just show up here with personality traits. I love to ask little toddlers who are only beginning to communicate with language to tell me what they remember about their experiences before coming here for this earthly incarnation. In fact, this entire book was created because my co-author, Dee Garnes, engaged in such a conversation with her little boy, Marcus, who was just learning how to communicate in single words. (You can read about this joyful conversation in Dee's Introduction, which follows mine.)

I have asked adults from all walks of life to share the wisdom of their little ones, and I have included many of my own experiences with my children's recollections in this book. After reading through the responses that Dee and I received from people all over the planet, I am more than convinced that there is much more to our lives than the few short years we are allotted here on Earth. And our young boys and girls are the ones who can offer us a glimpse into the unfathomable, infinite, invisible world that is for all of us to discover. After all, they haven't had much time to truly forget.

I have always loved the poem written by the English poet William Wordsworth, titled "Ode: Intimations of Immortality from Recollections of Early Childhood." One of the lines says: "Our birth is but a sleep and a forgetting." As I would look into the eyes of one of my own newborns, I would frequently contemplate what the poet is saying here. This entire human experience is like a dream: we sleep, we dream, and then we awaken, forgetting all of those wondrous experiences in our dream state. But sometimes we can recall some tidbits of that dream, particularly if we have very recently emerged from sleep. As I would look at this newly arrived miracle in my lap, I'd feel the truth of Wordsworth's words.

Our birth may indeed be a sleep, but not all of it is forgotten by children, and it was thanks to that idea that this compilation was born. Every remembrance cited here came from children who seem to have these recollections, just as we adults do when attempting to explain what has taken place in that mysterious dream world we enter every night, and live in for at least one-third of our time here.

Dee and I have gone through thousands upon thousands of entries that were sent to us when we asked for personal anecdotes about young children's memories of heaven. So many of the stories that my own children relayed to me when they were just learning to talk, which I thought were unique to me and our family, have actually turned out to be quite universal in nature—countless people gave us almost identical stories about children reporting how they remembered choosing their parents for this journey, how they had invisible friends that only they could see, memories of past lives in the same family, visitations with God, and on and on.

Today there is an entire literature filled with rigorous scientific evidence of past lives and the presence of angels among us. I myself have had a very powerful journey to a previous life, and I have had my mind expanded by my close association with many highly respected scholars who have provided convincing testimony for the reality of the infinite spiritual realm. But it is out of the mouths of these babes, who have recently shown up here and still have some remnants of heaven clinging to them—which they talk about unequivocally—that we are all provided with clues to the world beyond. It is to those voices that this book is dedicated.

In Wordsworth's "Recollections of Early Childhood" he gives us this to chew on as well: "The Soul that rises with us, our life's Star, / Hath had elsewhere its setting, / And cometh from afar . . . From God, who is our home." As you read through these enthralling commentaries about the world beyond what we see and experience with our five senses, know that these little beings are drenched in the heaven that is our home. They have so much to teach us all.

BY DEE GARNES

Dr. Wayne Dyer and I have been great friends for many years. We started off as neighbors, followed by him becoming one of my massage clients, and then I began working for him as his assistant. Ever since the birth of my son, Marcus, Wayne has encouraged me to ask him questions, such as if he remembers God or what heaven is like. From that advice, this book began.

Marcus was 18 months old, and I was pregnant with my second child, Shiloh. We were at the table for dinner, starting off with my favorite childhood prayer: "Thank you for the world so sweet. Thank you for the food we eat. Thank you for the birds that sing. Thank you, God, for everything."

As we began to eat, I was staring with pride at this stunning little miracle by my side who was fumbling around with his fork, giddy with excitement and beaming with pride every time he managed to actually feed himself. He was glowing with his blond curly locks, deep green eyes, and perfect skin. I remember putting a hand on my protruding belly and feeling so incredibly blessed. So many questions came to me about these lives that my husband, Trey, and I had created (I am still so amazed that these beautiful little creatures are my babies).

I recall how mystified Trey and I had been months before when Marcus had placed his tiny hands on my belly, patting me gently, and declared, "Baby! Baby!" I'd had no idea that I was pregnant with Shiloh; in fact, I couldn't have been pregnant for more than a day or two. Yet Marcus, in his infinite wisdom, sensed this beginning miracle growing within me and announced it with absolute certainty.

As I was gazing at my boy now, I was thinking to myself, *Somehow I made this little boy, all his physical parts . . . but where did he come from? How did he develop this consciousness?* Anyone who has been around babies and children will agree that their presence here is beyond mysterious. Without even thinking, I blurted out with awe, "Where did you come from?" I wasn't expecting an answer; Marcus only knew a few words. To my surprise, he dropped his fork, looked up, and raised both of his arms to the sky. Wow.

That prompted the next question, which Wayne had inspired me to ask: "What is God like?" Marcus looked directly into my eyes, and so simply and casually replied in his sweet angelic voice, "Light."

At that moment, I understood that the little boy sitting next to me and the teeny baby in my belly were so much more than just their small bodies. They had souls that contained wisdom from beyond this earthly realm, which was far beyond my comprehension. *If we just listen,* I realized, *they have so much to teach us all.*

I shared this story with Wayne the next day, and he encouraged me to write it down. I did so while sitting in the doctor's office at one of my prenatal appointments. With my permission, Wayne posted the story on his Facebook page, inviting others to share their personal experiences as well. The responses and comments poured in, and that is how the idea for this book began.

My role with *Memories of Heaven* was to gather all of the stories and then organize them into chapters. I was quite intimidated by this, as there were thousands of contributions and I had no idea what type of category I would to put them in. Yet as I read each submission, it was easy to see that the chapters presented themselves.

Wayne and I then got together about every two weeks to work on a chapter. We went over each story, reading them out loud; he'd then take that chapter home and meditate on it for the next week or two. Then he would write his introduction and suggestions for that chapter.

I have read countless stories and spoken to many parents who have shared the words of wisdom and remembrances of their young ones. It was quite a journey reading these vignettes while being pregnant and having a toddler. All of it taught me to, as Wayne says, "Have a mind that is open to everything and attached to nothing." I found that in fact angels do exist. Imaginary friends are better described as "invisible friends." Deep-rooted wisdom perhaps originates from past experiences, not from this lifetime. Some of us actually choose our parents or family members. The possibilities are endless.

As I am writing this, my now-two-year-old, Marcus, is asleep on my right; my eight-week-old, Shiloh, is asleep on my left; and the words of Charles Dickens resonate with me: "I love little children, and it is not a slight thing when they, who are fresh from God, love us." I feel so fortunate and blessed to be in the presence of these two bundles of love. And to think that they chose me to be their mother makes me feel immensely honored.

A wise woman I recently met shared this saying with me: "When we enter this world, we are crying and everyone is laughing. When we leave this world, we are laughing and everyone is crying." Perhaps the reason babies cry is because they miss where they came from. If we just listen with an open heart and mind to our little ones, we can learn so much from them—and possibly help our future generations to not forget where they came from, as well as the incredible, exciting journey that lies beyond this physical one.

MEMORIES OF
HEAVEN

One of my very favorite passages from *A Course in Miracles* reads like this:

> The memory of God comes to the quiet mind.
> It cannot come where there is conflict, for
> a mind at war against itself remembers not
> eternal gentleness. . . . What *you* remember
> *is* a part of you. . . . Let all this madness be
> undone for you, and turn in peace to the
> remembrance of God, still shining in your
> quiet mind.

Each of the stories that appear in this first chapter are remembrances of little boys and girls who have not progressed far enough along this ego-dominated earthly plane to have a mind that is at war against itself. In essence, all of these children who give evidence of having memories of an existence prior to arriving here have quiet minds. Their minds are not filled with doubts, which lead to conflicts about what they feel inwardly versus what they're being told by so many adults—who themselves have forgotten the eternal gentleness that once shone in their own quiet minds.

A quiet mind is one that is willing to speak the truth that is felt internally. It is a mind that has not yet been conditioned to accept a reality that is being imposed upon it by well-meaning adults and cultural and religious teachings. All of the offerings in this chapter came out of the mouths of young children, who appear to have convincing knowledge of their existence prior to arriving here in this corporeal realm that we call reality.

The statements offered here are a sampling of thousands of such comments that Dee and I received from parents and relatives from all over our planet. I have a quiet mind that has obviously done a lot of forgetting about my life prior to my birth, but it is a mind that is open to everything, a mind that does not fully grasp the idea of infinity yet is open to the idea that in an infinite universe, there is no room for beginnings and endings . . . infinite means always, and therefore there is an invisibleness within and surrounding us all that is beginningless and endless. It is obviously not our physical form that I refer to here;

it is that formless space within that can never die, and is never born.

It is here where young children have the advantage. They speak their truth and recall their remembrances without any concern for what anyone else might think about it. For example, when she was a young child, my own daughter Serena while sleeping would literally converse in a language that was foreign to everyone in our family. She would offer recollections of her previous lives, and on one occasion informed my wife that "You are not my real mother. I have a real mother that I remember, but it's not you."

As you read these stories, I encourage you to practice something that I learned from a 10th-century scholar in India named Tilopa. His advice was to "have a mind that is open to everything and attached to nothing." Allow yourself to turn in peace to the memory of God, which is possibly still shining in your own quiet mind.

One of the most profound and life-changing moments of my life came when my oldest son was eight years old.

Sean had always been a sensitive child with wide eyes, a heart as big as the sun, and a smile that could light up the room. I had been the type of mother who loved her son and fulfilled of all his physical needs, but I always felt a missing connection—a bond I so desperately wanted yet didn't know how to obtain. At the time, I didn't have the spiritual or energetic awareness to define it; I simply knew that Sean could feel this missing bond. I tried to compensate by taking good care of him and showering him with affection, but I was overly controlling and angry. I didn't want to be that way and tried not to be, but it's like this impulse had a life of its own.

My controlling manner was on overdrive one particular day, and that evening when I tucked Sean into bed, he began to sob uncontrollably. As compassionately as I could, I asked him what was the matter, and he said that he wanted his mother in heaven. I inquired what he meant by that, and he told me that he just wanted to be with his mother in heaven and couldn't take it being here. This began to scare me, but I gently asked him what his mother in heaven gave him that I didn't. He said, "Pure love."

I could feel my heart begin to soften as I looked at my son in so much pain, missing something he so deserved, and there was no doubt in my mind that what he was telling me was real. As I continued to talk with him, he explained how his mother in heaven, along with God, told him to pick me for his earthly mother, and that he remembered being inside me and it was dark.

I asked Sean if he recalled what God looked like, and he described Him as a being of white light and full of love. I knew in this moment that Sean had just given me, and himself, a gift: a remembering from this little boy who wanted his mother to give him "pure love"! I knew he picked me as his mother to help me learn how to experience and express pure love and for him to receive it from me, his mother right now. This day began the journey of awakening the Divine mother in me right here on Earth!

— **ROBIN LISA HAYWOOD**
Union, Kentucky

When my daughter, Sarenna, was just under two years of age, she was very verbal. She would look me in the eyes and tell me how happy she was to be with me—how much she missed me when she was waiting to come to Earth to be with me, how she had watched me from the Other Side, so excited for the time when she could come join me. It still takes my breath away when I think about it.

Sarenna was (and still is) a very peaceful and easygoing child. She rarely became upset growing up, but the few times she did, she would cry that she wanted "to go home." Most of the time we were actually at our house, so I asked her what she meant. She explained that she wanted to go back home, the place where she was before she came to live here in this life. She referred to heaven as "home." I would hug her and let her know it was all right, that we are here together. She is such a sweet kid, and so wise. I feel very blessed/honored to be here with her.

— **NATASHA WESTRICH WOOD**
Ballwin, Missouri

About a year ago, my daughter and I were playing with a rose-quartz stone. She was happy holding the stone and then got sad. I asked her what was wrong, and she said, "I miss God." I asked her why, and she began to explain to me that when she was in her dragon's cave (that's what she named the womb), she spoke with God all the time. She said, "He was pure love." Sometimes, she told me, she would have wings, and "God was always love and it felt so nice."

I explained that God was still with her. She got happier and raised her head to the sky, then looked at me and said, "I know, Mamma. God is here with us now. I just miss always talking to God." I said, "Well, don't stop . . . you can talk with God whenever you want."

My daughter is now three and a half, and not a day goes by when she doesn't have some story or interaction with God. It is so powerful and humbling!

— **CARLY JEANNE**
Fallon, Nevada

Years ago when my three girls were little, I put the two youngest ones to bed, telling them to lie there quietly and go to sleep. Molly was five years old, and Caroline was not yet two at the time. More than an hour after I'd put them to bed, I heard giggling and talking coming from the bedroom, so I made my way to the back of the house to admonish them for not going to sleep.

As I approached the bedroom, I stopped short when I heard Molly ask Caroline if she still remembered what it was like before she was born. "Yes," replied Caroline. "I 'member picking Mommy, Daddy, Liana, and you! I could see you from up there! And I saw Grandma and Grandpa, too. They were smiling! I see'd everything!"

"Oh yeah," said Molly slowly. "Caroline, I'm starting to forget . . ."

"I know."

Both remained oddly quiet and still for several moments after this, until Molly began making faces and acting silly, as she often did when trying to get her little sister to laugh and play.

— **MAUREEN SUHADOLNIK**
Springfield, Illinois

When my son, Casey, was around three or four years old, he seemed to have moments of struggling with depression. One day I was trying to find out what was bothering him, and he told me he "just wanted to go home." I said, "What do you mean? You are home." He said he used to live with God and wanted to go back, and it was hard to live here.

When I asked him what it was like with God, he said it felt like home and you could always play and nothing bad ever happened. He continued to have this same type of conversation with me off and on for a few months, and I made sure to listen very carefully each time.

Casey is a happy, sensitive, playful, energetic ten-year-old now. Whatever was going on back then, it definitely seemed to help him just to talk about it.

I should also mention that he was a colicky baby, and I often wondered if that was because he was having a hard time adjusting to this world.

— **JENNIFER MOORE**
Niles, Michigan

When my son Joseph was five, he broke his arm trying to "fly" off the top of his brother's cot. I walked into the room to find Joseph crying, so I brought him up onto my knee for a cuddle and asked, "What's wrong?" He just looked at me with wide eyes and asked, "Mum, when am I going to get my wings back?" When I told him that as a human he wouldn't have wings but could fly kites and planes and so on, he burst into tears and wailed, "I want them right now!" All I could do was hug him. Then he gulped, suddenly stopped crying, looked straight into my eyes, and said, "That's okay, Mum, I remember God told me I could have them when I returned after this assignment."

Then there's my granddaughter, Phoebe. She was four when my mother died, and everyone had tried to explain to her why I was sad. She climbed on my lap and asked, "Where's Supernana?" I told her that my mother had died and gone to heaven. Phoebe said, "So she is with God and the angels?" I replied, "Yes." She thought about it for a while and then climbed down, stood in front of me with her hands on her hips, and asked one final question: "So why are you still sad?" Even now when the grief occasionally arises, I hear this question and my granddaughter's logic, and I am immediately filled with joy.

A few days later she again climbed on my lap. "I'm happy you're not so sad now, Nana Sue," she said. "'Cause you know even as we talk, Supernana might be getting ready to come back as a baby. You know, they call it a big word that starts with an 'R.'" I said, "Reincarnation?" She replied, "That's right, that's what God said."

— **SUSAN LOVEJOY**
Coffs Harbor, New South Wales, Australia

I was babysitting my granddaughter, Kira, who was just over a year old. I was changing her diaper, when she looked at me and said, "I want to go home." I explained to her how we had to wait for her mom and dad to come and pick her up. Later when her parents were back, I said how she missed them and wanted to go home, and their response was, "She says the same thing when she's *at* home."

— **MARY GUSTAFSON**
Alberta, Canada

My son, Michael, has PDD (pervasive developmental disorder), and sometimes navigating the world is difficult for him. Yet throughout his nine years, he has made more than one declaration about God and heaven. For example, just two days ago, completely unprompted, he began talking about how he helped God decide who his sisters would be before they came here. He said that God is sparkling white and before babies are born, He puts a bright blue light inside them, which is always there. He said that everyone in heaven is young like children, it is "all love," and there are angels everywhere.

Michael's ability to articulate all of this was breathtaking—a reminder that God is always with him, even if I don't see it due to the challenges he faces.

— **TRISH SULLIVAN**
Bernardsville, New Jersey

My family was created through adoption. My son, Parker Jose (PJ), was adopted from Guatemala when he was ten months old. He was born with a congenial heart condition, so within the first month, he had an operation to correct his patent ductus arteriosus (PDA), which is a hole in the heart that should close at birth. PJ was a very good-natured child who didn't cry when the nurses and doctors stuck him with IVs, gave him shots, and took his blood. The health-care workers could not believe how agreeable he was for an ill child. He had four operations before the age of five.

My daughter, Sedona, who was adopted from China, is three years older than PJ. I've always said prayers and sung with both of them at bedtime; when PJ began to talk as a toddler, he would tell Sedona and me about heaven. He told us that God is very nice, and that he knew that he was going to be healthy because God promised him. He talked about heaven's beauty, how there were all these vibrant colors, especially in the flowers. When he was telling us these stories, Sedona would be looking at him questioning his statements. She'd move her finger round and round to indicate that he was crazy, as kids do.

When PJ had his final heart surgery, the cardiologist told us that the operation was not a complete success as there was nothing they could do to completely close the hole. The hole was in the center of his heart, so it was unlikely to heal, and PJ would have to take precautions to avoid a fatal heart infection for the rest of his life. However, a year after the last operation, his annual echocardiogram showed a different story. A miracle had occurred!

PJ remembered God's promise to him and, of course, he was right. He is now a healthy 13-year-old. God is good!

— **SANDI WILSON**
Phoenix, Arizona

I had just returned from a weekend retreat in which I was totally immersed in Spirit, when my four-year-old grandson climbed up on my lap. Snuggling as close as he could, he looked me in the eyes and very seriously said, "I am forgetting how to fly."

It was a profound moment in my life, and I have never forgotten it. My grandson taught me the truth of where we come from and who we are within. This truth is so easily forgotten in the business of living on this planet. Consistent meditation and prayer time help me to remember "how to fly."

— **TRINA LEMBERGER**
O'Fallon, Missouri

My Chloe, who is four, talks about seeing "Dead people in my behind eye"—she came up with that expression all on her own. She has told me that before she was born, she remembers sitting in a circle with her angel brothers and sisters and her angel mom, and they were playing with a ball. She says that was the last time she saw them, and she's sad because she really misses her angel family.

— **MEGAN FARLEY TUCKER***

My mother had two miscarriages before my sister was born. When my sister was three, she told Mum that she could remember playing with her other two sisters in heaven and was sad she couldn't play with them on Earth as they were "good fun." She also told Mum that they are really happy up there!

— **AMY ELISABETH RATTIGAN**
New Taipei City, Taiwan

I took my three young children to a children's fair at the park. One of the activities was an art project in which paper was attached to record players that were spinning at low speeds, and children could select bottles of paint and squirt the paper as it went round and round. My three-year-old son, David, chose yellow, blue, and orange, and created a beautiful sunburst. He handed it to me and said, "This is for you, Mom. This is me when I was sunshine with God before I was born."

This happened 21 years ago, and that sunburst still takes my breath away when I look at it.

— LINDA SMITH
Richland, Washington

My son, Christian, died in 1996 when he was 14 months old from an undiagnosed rare cancer. After he died, I had a miscarriage. I prayed to my son to send us a child that would be perfect for our family.

I got pregnant again in 1997, and the doctor told me that I had a false pregnancy: all the symptoms and no heartbeat. She assured me that I would not need to go through the same painful dilation and curettage (D & C) that I'd had to with the last miscarriage. I would return to the office in a few weeks for an injection that would eliminate the need for the D & C. I had a very strong feeling not to do this. I called a nurse-practitioner that I know, and she said that some pregnancies can be too early to detect a heartbeat and that repeating the sonogram in a few weeks wouldn't hurt.

My husband and I prayed and accepted what we felt was God's will. The injection was scheduled for the same day as the sonogram, and when we walked into the room, the technician made sure to turn the monitor away from us. When we were told to see the radiologist in the next room, I asked my husband to wait in the car, but the technician insisted that he come with me. The radiologist put a film on the board and with his finger outlined a baby—he had also detected the heartbeat! We sat there and cried knowing that was the day we were supposed to have the injection. Had I not listened to that voice inside me, my beautiful daughter would not be here.

I had a picture in my living room of my husband holding Christian on the only Christmas we'd had with him. One day my then-three-year-old daughter pointed to his picture and said, "I know him." I told her that he died before she was born, so she'd never meet him. She replied, "I know him from before I was born." I just cried. She is such a miracle to us, and even at age 16 is so special and clearly tuned in to that voice inside her.

— **SHERYL REYES-CUEVAS**
Lehigh Acres, Florida

My daughter is the youngest of four children. She has maintained, since about the age of three, how much she missed each brother when they left to be born. We would all stifle a giggle when she told this story. She is 13 now and well educated in science, and she says she still remembers saying good-bye to each of her brothers. They are so close as siblings, even though they're years apart in age . . . fascinating stuff.

— **TAMMY SHAW**
Brooklyn, New York

My husband and I lost our first daughter, Beth, due to heart problems when she was almost three years old. Our third daughter, Amy, born five years after this, hadn't been told about Beth. When she was about three and a half, we pulled out a video of Beth, and Amy said, "That's my sister Beth! I knew her in heaven before I was born."

— **PAULA CONROY**
Gloucester City, New Jersey

My daughter was three, and I was tucking her into bed after story time. I told her how glad I was to be her mommy, and she looked at me very seriously and said that she paid God thunderbolts and lightning to get me as her mom. Okay, that was cute, but then she said, "And

I remember that my head hurt over here." She pointed to the exact spot where her head had been stuck in the birth canal. I never told her about her delivery because she was so young, and I was completely amazed. She kept repeating the lightning and thunderbolt story—she is now 30 and, boy, is she the stormy one!

— **ROBIN WILLIS**
Granada Hills, California

My father (Grandpa Jones) passed away in the spring of 1998, and my granddaughter was born that fall. When she was about two years old, Afton was sitting in her car seat, looking out at my mother, who was standing near the car. My granddaughter said, "I'm so sad for her because she lost the one she loved and is so sad."

Afton's parents quizzed her on how she would have known that, and showed her a picture of Grandpa Jones when they arrived home. She said, "Oh, I know him . . . I talked to him before I came here!"

We were all so thrilled to hear those remarks from Afton, as she was fairly fresh from heaven and very emphatic about what she was talking about.

— **DARLENE**
Melita, Manitoba, Canada

When my son, Dustin, was around two years of age, we were riding around in the car and he hit himself on the forehead with his hand—kind of like the commercial that states, "I could've had a V8." And he said, "Mama, I'm starting to forget what heaven looks like." Needless to say, it gave me chills.

— **SHERRI JUNKINS**
Greenville, South Carolina

My two-year-old never wavered in her conviction that I was pregnant with her brother. My husband and I chose not to find out, but I didn't want her to be disappointed. So I said, "We may be having a girl."

"No!" declared my daughter. "I met him in heaven before I was born."

She was right—we had a boy!

— **KELSEA ZOULAMIS**
Richmond, Maine

My daughter, Alissa, was born in 1998, and both of her paternal grandparents had died in the early 1980s. One day we were driving in the car, and my very bright and verbal two-year-old told me that she saw her grandparents, and she knew them when she was in heaven with God. This made the hair on the back of my neck stand up, and just confirmed everything I believe.

— **CASSANDRA GIOVANATTO**
Cloverdale, California

My grandfather was the true patriarch of our family. He was often sought out in the neighborhood for advice and such, and was a wise and kind Navy veteran who was the captain of a ship in World War II. He had a long, painful decline due to a brain tumor, and his passing was a great loss.

My three-year-old niece had never met my grandfather, although she may have heard of him around the table or seen photos. One day she said something about him to her mother (who is not into past lives or the like). My sister-in-law, who had never met him either, said, "Oh yes, Boompa, your great-grandfather. You haven't met him, but you have seen his picture."

My niece remarked, "Yes, I have, Mommy. I was with him when he was sick, and he was with me before I came down." My sister-in-law had her repeat what she said and then called her husband, my brother, shaking. We were all so shocked!

— **AMY STEINMAN**
Wayne, Pennsylvania

When my son was about four years old, we took him shopping to a Walmart that we had never been to before. An elderly black man greeted us at the door with a smile, saying, "Hello! Welcome to Walmart."

My son got so excited. He threw his hand up and waved, and replied exuberantly, "Heyyyyyy! How *are* you?!" He said it as if he were greeting an old friend he hadn't seen in years. (He was usually very shy of strangers, so this caught me off guard.) Then without missing a beat, he looked at me enthusiastically and said, "He was my friend. I knew him when I was in heaven with God."

I was totally speechless, as was the elderly man.

— **KIMBERLIE HAWKINS**
Albrightsville, Pennsylvania

One day my three-year-old nephew was in the car and the song "Only Sixteen" by Sam Cooke came on the radio. He said, "Oh, Grandpa loves Sam Cookie." Well, his grandpa had died many years before my nephew had been born, but he was right—Sam Cooke was one of my dad's favorite singers. I asked his parents if they ever discussed this with him and they said no, so I figure that before my nephew was born he spent time with his grandpa. That gives me a lot of peace and happiness.

— **MARY HIRSCH**
Minneapolis, Minnesota

I have four children, all of whom were brought up in a fairly spiritual home. My youngest, Abigail (now age 30), was premature by several weeks at birth. When I held her for the first time, I felt that she was special. It's not that she was any better than her siblings, but is special in a sort of unexplainable way.

Abs grew up like most children under five, asking questions that make us parents wish we had studied the encyclopedia before their conception . . . however, her questionings and spiritual comments baffled me somewhat, even left me questioning my faith and belief. Then one day out of the blue, as were walking down the road to my "Women of Faith" class, she blurted out, "And when I was in heaven before I was born . . ." She was around three. I have not forgotten those words and never will! I sort of chuckled to hide my surprise and asked her what she meant. She just continued to talk about God, and pretty things and big light, and coming down into Mummy's tummy. She also spoke some about what it was like to live in Mummy's tummy. I dismissed the conversation, reflecting on the class ahead of us. (At that time I was a spiritual teacher and the local preacher.)

To my surprise, Abigail announced when she was four years old that she was going to be the preacher at our church when she was seven. As anyone who knows us will confirm, she started to study the Bible and to ask many spiritual questions. Then by the age of five, she had added the dictionary to her study time. And as sure as her prophecy, on her seventh birthday she was our youngest preacher to date.

I will never forget that Sunday when we placed our baby up on the chair in front of the congregation and handed her the microphone, and listened to her speak from a place that was within her. We clapped so hard and praised her so much, yet she only preached one more time: when she was ten, she wrote a piece on "What is love?" for a midweek service. As she went on to secondary school, she became less and less interested.

— **REV. DAWNECIA PALMER, AKA APOSTLE GRATEFUL**
Fishponds, Bristol, United Kingdom

As a small child, I had a clear memory of watching my parents before birth: I was looking down at them from above as they sat in a park. Years later my mom and I were talking, and she mentioned their favorite spot in a park, which they had gone to as a young married couple.

I asked her to take me there, and it was the exact spot from my memories.

— **LOLA BRADY EVERETT**
Fairfax, Virginia

My son was about four or five and we were eating lunch, when out of the blue he said, "Mommy, after God made me and before I was born, I knew I was going to be happy. I just didn't know what toys I would have." This blew me away because we were not talking about God or religion, and he came up with this out of thin air.

— **KIM HERGERT**
West Boylson, Massachusetts

I was raised very religious and chose to let my daughter, Angel'lina, hear about God when she was older. However, she spoke about angels and orbs often, and saw auras and colors—I was so fascinated by how she would sit and laugh and ask me if I saw them, too. Her explanation was that they were floating balls of light!

When Angel'lina was five, she was diagnosed with ADHD. One day she burst into tears and said, "Why did God have to make this world so hard? I just want to be with God and the angels!" This was not the only time she had referred to being upset with God and how the world was—she was so aware of how nasty some of the world could be. One day I said, "I love you so much," and she said, "I love you more." Then I said, "Well, I loved you first, when you were in my tummy," and she said, "Nope, I loved you first when I was in heaven waiting to get into your tummy."

My child is what brought me back to spirituality—I had fallen away from church when I was 15—I found a way to express my beliefs and spirituality through her. I wouldn't have had any idea how powerful God's messengers were and how they had been guiding me all this time, had she not sparked my curiosity.

— **CARLY JO SANFILIPPO**
Cambridge, Ontario, Canada

My mother's identical twin sister, Faye, had died when they were 23 years old. They were best friends, of course; they had leaned on each other even more than regular identical twins because of their very difficult childhood.

My daughter, Julia, was a very chatty toddler, as many little girls are! One day my mom asked her if she knew who Faye was. Julia replied, "Yes, I was swinging with her in the clouds before I came. We were picking out my family and wearing pretty white dresses." No one had told Julia about Faye because she was only a baby—how could she possibly understand?

— **JANIS MONACHINA**
Lee, Massachusetts

One day my husband and I were talking to our son about his grandfathers and showing him their photos, as they had passed before he could meet them. Our son was about 3 years old at that time (he's now 15), and he told us that he had met my husband's father on his way here. His words were, "I know him—he's Poppy Henry. I saw him on my way to you."

— **MICHELE MIRA**
Stamford, Connecticut

My nephew, who was three years old at the time, told me he was in a big chair watching his mommy cry, and "she needed someone to love, so I became her baby." I was amazed!

— **APRIL RANDLETT DUCHENEAU**
Dracut, Massachusetts

My four-year-old used to talk about when he was in heaven before he was born, and when I asked him what it was like, he said it was all parks.

— **RAINA THORSEN**
Staten Island, New York

When my son was very young, he told me about the "getting-born game." He said that he and a few of his friends were in a big church up in the clouds before they were born. They were crawling in a circle around a hole in the floor, and the floor was made of clouds. There was beautiful music playing. Every now and then the music would stop, and one of the friends would go down the hole and get born.

I didn't take him to church when he was little, so this story was especially surprising to me.

— **JOANN RICHMOND HINKSMON**
Hamberg, New Jersey

When I was in my early 20s, I was a nanny for a two-and-a-half-year-old boy. One late summer day, I took him to the park, which was filled with fuzzy dandelions. We sat down and proceeded to blow the fuzz off them, filling the air with seeds. Suddenly, he stopped blowing, looked down at the stem in his chubby little hand, and said, "I used to be the god of these." I was stunned. I said, "What was that like?" But he just got up and ran off into the flying dandelion fuzz.

I have never forgotten the mystery, innocence, and power of that moment.

— **LISA FAIRMAN**
Ramsey, New Jersey

When my daughter, Angelica, was close to 3 years old (she's now 20), we were driving and just having a conversation. She said, "Mommy, I love you to the moon and back again," which we said often to each other, so that wasn't out of the ordinary. I was joking with her and asked if she'd ever been to the moon. She said no. I said, "That is a long way, like up in heaven—have you ever been to heaven?" She said yes.

"You have? My mommy is in heaven, and I am sorry that you never got to meet her."

"Yes, I did."

"What do you mean?"

Angelica said, "I saw her in heaven with God."

What my daughter said sent chills up and down my body—just the way the conversation was so casual and sort of grown-up, yet how easily it came out of her mouth. I will never forget that day.

— **BARB O'ROURKE**
Boca Raton, Florida

This story may seem unreal, which is why I haven't told many people except for close family members. About 15 years ago, I already had three children, who by this time were between 11 and 15 years old. I was "told" I was going to have two babies to take care of, and the "voice" I was hearing referred to them as Grace and Noah. I kept getting this message over and over again for about five months.

I was not trying to get pregnant; in fact, quite the opposite. Nevertheless, I found out I was pregnant. I thought I must be having twins, right? No, just one— so I didn't put much stock in my voices. I had a girl, and even though I wasn't really sure about my voices, I did make her middle name Grace (just in case).

Nine months later, I got pregnant again and had a boy. His middle name is Noah.

Here's a bit of background on my daughter: She is exceptional, using sign language to communicate at six months old and reading at age two. I always called her by her first name, but when she was two, she told me that she had always been Grace and that's what "everyone else" called her, too. She said, "God calls me Grace, so do Grandma and Grandpa in heaven, and so does Noah."

I asked if she saw God now, because I wasn't sure how this was possible, and she said no. She left God and her grandparents and Noah to come be with me, but she was happy because Noah wanted to come here to be with us, too. (He was about eight months old at the time.)

My daughter told me she was in heaven before her birth and remembered times there. She remembered it like it was just another day. Sorry to say we didn't go to church, so she didn't really have any knowledge at that time of who God was . . . or so I thought.

— **RHONDA THOMPSON**
Fairfield, Iowa

My children used to refer to a time before they "came down," which I interpreted as meaning before they took human form. They spoke as though they were in a place above us and could look down and see what was happening down there. I used to love it when they spoke of it!

— **CATHY SCHANZE**
Gilbert, Arizona

❦ I suggest that you begin to view any of the young children in your life as new arrivals from heaven. Communicate with them by asking questions about their recollections. Above all, do not dismiss anything that they might say, regardless of how absurd it may sound to you. Make an effort to engage your children in conversation, and rather than perceiving yourself as their teacher, allow them to take on that role with you. Be inquisitive and an active listener by drawing them out and taking a genuine interest in whatever they might offer.

Be aware that little ones, who are imparting those mysterious words that you might find difficult to grasp, speak their own unique truth. Let their honesty and excitement about these "weird" memories from heaven remind you that you too were once a small child, and that little child resides within you at all times.

It's important to never brush off or doubt these remembrances, and to keep in mind the famous observation of Mark Twain: "It ain't what you don't know that gets you into trouble. It's what you know for sure that just ain't so."

2

MEMORIES OF
PAST LIVES

⁂ I love these words spoken by Jesus in the New Testament: "See that you don't look down on one of these little ones, because I tell you that in heaven their angels continually view the face of My Father in heaven" (Matthew 18:10). They are particularly applicable as you read the passages that were sent to Dee and me from all over the world, detailing evidence of a life before coming to Earth this time. The words spoken by the children cited here seem to validate what is offered in the holy scriptures by Jesus Christ himself.

I have grappled with the great mysterious issues that have perplexed philosophers since the beginning of recorded history, and even before, if I can wager a guess about what humans discussed while residing in primitive caves. *Is there life before and after death? Are there really such a thing as angels? Is there a God, and if so, what does*

God look like? Do our souls and consciousness survive the death of our bodies? These are the enigmatic questions that have always puzzled scholars. However, the words spoken by so many of our young children may provide us with answers that have eluded the intellectual efforts of our wisest teachers. Entire books written by highly educated and respected scholars are indeed attesting to the truths spoken by our new arrivals.

All of the vignettes in this chapter are taken directly from the mouths of very young boys and girls—they speak of having lived in different bodies, of having died in an accident, of having been a grown-up in a previous lifetime, of having been a man with a wife before coming here. There is a growing body of evidence that is being subjected to rigid scientific examination procedures, which points to the fact of "life before life." This idea is now a verifiable conclusion by those who have studied this phenomenon in depth.

I have long held that children are much more than just biological beings being shaped by their genetic makeup and the environment in which they are immersed. They are essentially spiritual beings who bring with them wisdom and a host of experiences from having lived here in previous lifetimes. As you read these selections, you will become freed up from the fear of death and annihilation that so occupies the minds of most people on our planet. This is the single greatest fear that humans carry with them.

The awareness of the truths flowing from the mouths of our innocent children can offer an antidote to all of that unnecessary suffering, which is of immeasurable benefit.

Who we are is obviously not these bodies we inhabit. These physical shells are in a constant state of change, and we know for certain that everything that materializes will ultimately dematerialize. From all that we can gather from what our children tell us, our souls are indestructible, and they transcend time and space in a way that remains mysterious to all of us. Yes, our consciousness is infinite, meaning that it, unlike our bodies, is beginningless and endless. We are all infinite spiritual beings having a temporary human experience, and so many of our very special young ones are providing testimony to this grand idea.

I urge you to keep in mind the words of Jesus, and see that "you don't look down on one of these little ones."

When my eldest boy, Dawson, was between the ages of two and four, he would often give me details of a past life he lived. He began telling me about his "house in Asia." He talked about how he lived there with his sister and that the "house burned down in the war." He would talk repeatedly about a war, and this house in Asia and how it burned down.

One day, when he was a little closer to four, he was able to describe things in more detail. He told me that he "saw my sister in the house when it was burning." I asked him how he could see her, and he replied, "Because I was floating up above the house looking down. She died, too." Wow! He'd also often talk to me about things that she said. He described her as having long black hair and a strong face. I don't know if this was perhaps his sister from the past-life experience, or maybe a spirit guide or some other form of spiritual being. But I do know that he was too young to know of any such things as Asia, houses burning down, war, or people dying. It's beyond a shadow of a doubt in my mind that these were the memories of one of his past lives.

Dawson detailed multiple sightings of angels, and sometimes ghosts, as he grew older. He would also tell me things when he was young beginning with, "When I was an adult . . ." I was a believer in our spiritual nature before he was born, but his conversations with me when he was a young child validated my beliefs even more.

— **DOMINIQUE RYBA**
Vista, California

In 2005, my youngest child, Tristan, was four years old. I was in the kitchen cooking dinner, while he watched *Tom & Jerry* in the living room. During a commercial break, he came in and watched me for a moment with his little head cocked to one side. Out of the blue he said, "Do you remember a long time ago, I used to cook in George Washington's kitchen?"

I paused for a moment and asked, "You did?"

He nodded yes and then continued, "But I was a kid."

"Was I there?"

"Yes, you were a kid, too."

"Were we white people or black people?"

"We were brown people."

"Like Indians?"

He shrugged and then said, "But later I died," and he wrapped his little arms around his neck.

I asked, "What happened?"

"I couldn't breathe," he replied, then turned and went back into the living room.

The next day I Googled "George Washington's cook," and to my surprise a story and a photograph appeared. The man, named Hercules, had three children: Richmond, Evey, and Delia. His son, Richmond, went with his father to cook for Washington in Pennsylvania.

I asked Tristan that afternoon who Richmond was. He said, "Yes, I know him." So then I asked, "Do you know Evey?" and again was met with a yes. I asked if he knew Delia, but to that one he said no. He has since asked several times if we could go to Mount Vernon, but we have yet to make the trip.

— **RACHEL MARTIN**
Cherry Log, Georgia

When my son Cairo was born in 1993, I felt an immediate recognition and sense of remembering. It felt like I knew him somehow as a person, a sensation I never had with my firstborn, who felt like a beautiful new soul I had never met.

From the time he was very little, Cairo was always quite clingy with me. Wherever I went, he went, following me closely no matter what I did. He was a quite happy little boy who was always observing adults and never felt the need to speak a lot. He must have been about 22 months old when we were walking toward a road and I grabbed his hand tightly, telling him about the dangers of traffic and how he needed to hold my hand.

"Yeah," he said, very matter-of-factly, "otherwise I'll die again."

"Die again?" I was stunned as I looked at him.

"Yeah, 'member? When I was little and I fell and my head was on the road and the truck drove over it?"

I stood speechless, not only surprised by his sudden use of speech, but also trying to figure out where this bizarre and quite detailed remark came from. But he didn't blink an eye. He was very determined and serious. I asked him if he'd had a scary dream, a question that made him very offended.

"No-ho!" He spoke even louder, trying to get his point across. "When I was little and fell on the road and the truck drove over me, 'member?!" The fact that I didn't "'member" appeared to upset him the most. He kept staring at me insistently, frustrated as to how I could have forgotten. He mentioned something about pain, and then got distracted by other things.

I remember how my thoughts were racing. *Did he watch something on TV?* But we hardly watched TV and never anything gruesome like this. *Has there been anything on the news or in the papers? Is there anyone we know who recently died? Are there any stories going around that he may have picked up on?* For a split second, I did consider it could have been a past-life memory. Now I feel more certain that it was just that.

— **ELS VAN POPPEL**
Queensland, Australia

When my youngest son, J, was four or five, our family was sitting around the lunch table when he burst out angrily, "You are not my real mother!" Everyone was aghast. I asked him who his real mother was, and he told me her name was Colleen. I told him that Colleen was his mother before, but now I was his mother and was glad he came to be with us. That seemed to satisfy him because he never mentioned it again. No one in our family is named Colleen.

Now J's son, Jaiden, is seven. One day I took him to play in the Gold Star Garden (a veterans' memorial that I founded after my firstborn son, Martin, was killed in Iraq). That night as Jaiden was getting ready for bed, he told me that Martin looks out for him. "I know," I said. After all, Jaiden's middle name is Martin.

— **CHERRINEY KONDOR**
York, Pennsylvania

When my daughter was about three, she was sitting on my lap and we were singing a song. She was looking into my eyes and suddenly stopped singing. She kind of froze and spoke very slowly, asking me if I remembered the firehouse. She told me there was a fire, and her parents died in it. She described the scene, then said I was her Grandma Laura, and she came to live with me. She said she loved me so much in that lifetime. Then she stopped and went back to singing, probably because I had serious goose bumps, and I have to admit I was a little freaked out. At that time in my life I was still doing my best not to pay attention to spiritual things, yet my daughter already felt them deeply.

— **ANN MARIE GONZALEZ**
Sylmar, California

When my son was three years old, learning to tie his shoes, he looked up at me and said, "I used to be a man before, but I guess I will have to learn how to do this again."

— **SUSAN BOWERS**
Lancaster, South Carolina

When my son, Mark, was just about 3 years old (he's now 24), we were sitting down to read a book in his bed. He looked at me and out of the blue said, "I love you, Mommy, but did you know that you are not my real mommy?" He went on to tell me that his "real mommy, brother, and sister were all killed in a fire." I was totally shocked. He was so serious and further told me that he was scared, but the fireman saved him and God chose me to be his new mommy.

I told him, "No, Mark, I am your mommy." He looked at me with the most serious little face and said, "No, you are my other mommy, not my real mommy. I love you, but I miss them. I miss my brother and sister." Then he began to cry.

I'll never, ever forget it. And I'll never forget the look on his face when he told me, especially after I said no . . . I only wished I had asked him more about it. But honestly, he blew the wind out of my sails at the moment. I didn't know what to say or do, so I just held him tight and told him I loved him.

— **PAT McHUGH**
Worcester, Massachusetts

When my nephew was not quite two years old, he and I were in the car together and driving past some farmland in Florida. He was watching out the window, and when we passed a field with horses, clearly said, "I used to have a horse." Not knowing what to say, I chuckled and said, "You've never had a horse." He nodded and replied, "Yes, I did. But I fell off and broke my head." And with that, he quietly resumed looking out at the passing scenery. I could only get him to repeat this once more later that afternoon.

— **SHERRON WESTERFIELD**
Danville, Kentucky

When my sister-in-law, Erika, was about two or three years old, she asked her mother one day, "Isn't it true that we're all born and die over and over and over again?" Her mother didn't really know what to say to that. Later that afternoon they went to visit her grandmother, and Erika told her, "Grandma, I wish you would die." They were all shocked and asked her why she had just said that. She answered, "Because that way you could be born again, and you could go to school with me and we could be friends."

— **CECILIA SIANEZ**
Laredo, Texas

My second son, Ronnie, was talking at the age of 16 months, and I was privileged to hear in clearly spoken words the memories he had from before he was born. He would often mention another Mummy and Daddy and that he lived in a different house, telling us that he used to be a "grown-up."

The loveliest example of his closeness to his other life happened when I was reading *Autobiography of a Yogi* by Paramahansa Yogananda. Ronnie came up and asked what I was reading, and I told him it was a book written by a great spiritual teacher, a guru. I decided to show him all of the pictures in the book. When we got to a picture of Lahiri Mahasaya (1828–1895), a disciple of Babaji and guru to Paramahansa Yogananda's own guru, Sri Yukteswar, my son said, "Oh yeah, I know him." I asked, "How do you know him?" He replied, "I knew him before I came into your tummy."

It was at that moment that I realized the tiny toddler sitting next to me had a soul as old as mine. And despite me thinking that I was here to teach him something, I knew for certain that he was here to teach me just as much.

— **ZIBBY GUEST**
Chester, England

When Joseph, my middle son, was three years old, he was joyfully playing in our basement. He asked me, "Did you play with Play-Doh when you were a little girl?"

"No, they didn't have that when I was a little girl. They only had clay."

"Well, it's a lot of fun. So next time you're a little girl be sure to play with it." He must have seen the shocked look on my face because he said, "Oh, Mom, don't worry. You have a long time yet, but next time be sure to play with the Play-Doh." Then he smiled and continued to play.

The second incident happened around the same time period. He was sad when I put him to bed, so I asked, "What's wrong . . . what's bothering you?"

"I was just remembering my wife and how she died."

This time I knew not to looked shocked or upset, and instead replied, "What happened?"

He explained that he always wore a hat and what he described as painters' pants with the bib and the front straps. Please understand that we lived in the city of Philadelphia at the time, and he had no prior knowledge of what we would call painters' pants. His father was a policeman and never wore those kind of pants.

Joseph went on to tell me that he was crossing a bridge with his wife when she was attacked by bees. He said that she fell to the ground, and when he put his ear to her chest, he couldn't hear her heart bumping anymore—that was the explanation of a toddler. He said that he had many children and felt lost when his wife died. He wasn't asleep yet, and I saw the true sadness in his face. I just reassured him that she was in heaven and wasn't hurting anymore. That seemed to settle him down and allow him to go to sleep.

I know these aren't major stories, but 45 years later they are burned in my memory as if they happened yesterday.

— **CAROL GAIRO**
Bullhead City, Arizona

When my son, Kevin, was very young, he would often talk about the time when he "lived in the cottage house with the straw roof." He'd talk about how he was very old and sick, and spent most of his time sitting in a chair by the fire. The only time he would talk about being this person was when he was in a relaxed state, often just before going to sleep, and after about a month he stopped. He didn't seem to remember any of this if my wife and I quizzed him.

I did a bit of research on "cottage houses with straw roofs" and found they were usually built in medieval times in parts of Europe. I suspect that this memory was from near this person's end of life and perhaps that's why it carried over to this one.

My son is now almost 19 years old. While he still does not have any memory of his "past life," I find it interesting that he has a great interest in all things medieval.

— **TODD ST. CLAIR**
Prince Edward Island, Canada

My youngest saw a swastika and told me that she'd had it on her sleeve, which was a bad thing. She was a man in a bad war and had died, and she had a little girl with blonde hair and blue eyes. She said that she came here to make up for what she'd done before. She also used to hear voices, and it seemed to upset her when she found out that none of us heard them. So we prayed that they would go away until she was older and could understand better.

— **WENDY D. FIELDS**
Carney Point, New Jersey

My daughter shows tremendous memories of a life before this one. She started to speak fluently quite quickly, and on a few occasions has amazed me with her insight. Although my husband and I believe in past lives, we have never actively engaged her in conversation or spoken about it in her presence.

When my daughter was two years old, she and I were taking a bath together. She said to me, "Do you know, Mommy, in my other life I was the mom and you were the child, but you were a boy. You were very sick in bed and kept on crying for me. Only when I came to your bed were you able to die."

During that period she also touched my forehead. I asked her what she was doing. "I am touching your third eye, Mommy," she said. "Oh, and do all people have third eyes?" I replied. "Yes, but some people's third eye is closed, so they can't see," she answered. Neither my husband nor I had ever spoken about "third eyes."

When Nelson Mandela passed away, it was all over the news; and for us in South Africa, it was a tremendous loss. At the time, she was three years old, and we had a conversation in the car that unfolded as follows.

Daughter: Who is this "Madiba"?

Me: He was a very important man who taught us peace and brought people together. He died and now people are sad.

Daughter: Was he old?

Me: Yes, he was old.

Daughter: Then why are people sad? It was his time to go. Besides, he'll come back as a baby again.

— **AN-LI**
South Africa

In 1998 I was babysitting a very good friend's two-year-old daughter, Christina. Once everyone had left, Christina and I were sitting on the living-room floor watching cartoons. I was lying down, and she was leaning back on me watching the TV. All of the sudden, she turned around and looked at me and said, "The last time I died was because of my heart." Then she just went back to watching TV again. I was so surprised by her comment I didn't even know what to say, so I asked her to repeat it. She turned around again and said, "The last time I died was because of my heart." Even though I wanted to know more, I didn't prod her because I wanted whatever she told me to be spontaneous, on her own. When her mom came home, I told her about what happened, and she too was amazed that a little girl could articulate such a statement.

A few years went by, and Christina was about five years old and had moved into a brand-new house. When I went over for a visit, of course she wanted to show me her beautiful new bedroom. When we got there, she pointed out different things that she loved about her room. There was a picture of her mom sitting on her nightstand, and I said, "Oh, Christy, I love that picture of your mom," to which she replied, "Yeah, she looks like my last mom; her name was Rita. Their hair was the same." Again, I didn't know what to say!

When my own daughter, Julia, was about four, she began telling me about the family she had "last time." She told me, "My mom's name was Kalencia, my sister's name was Katy, I had a brother named Junior, but I don't know my dad's name. He was a bad guy, and we weren't allowed to talk about him." She went on to say that she "lived in a pink house, and it was in Florida." These were all the details she offered about the life she had lived before the life she has now.

A few weeks later, I came home from work and found a piece of paper on my husband's nightstand. Written on the paper in my husband's handwriting were the names *Kalencia, Katy,* and *Junior.* The phrase *Pink house, in Florida* was also on the note. I took the paper to my husband and asked why he had written those things down. He said that our daughter had told him the same exact story that she had told me. I thought it was interesting that a four-year-old would remember the name Kalencia, as I had never heard it before, but

Julia told both her dad and me the exact same story several weeks apart.

I have always sensed that my daughter could see beyond the veil.

— TRACEY GOOD JOWERS
Conroe, Texas

When my youngest was little, she would cry and scream whenever she heard sirens. Finally, one day I asked her why she'd get so upset. She told me that one time a siren came and took away her mommy, and her mommy never came back. I told her that I was her mom and I was fine. She said, "No, the mommy before you."

Also, she is obsessed with the *Titanic*. One day I showed her the movie and she started crying hysterically and told me that she was on that ship and died in the water.

— HEATHER LEIGH SIMPSON
Indianapolis, Indiana

We were at the dinner table the other night and I asked my boyfriend's daughter, who is going to be four in a week, about her upcoming birthday. I asked her how old she was going to be. She said, "Ten." I said, "Ten, huh? I thought you were going to be four." Then she said, "I was ten before, and now I'm going to be four . . . one, two, three, four, five, six, seven, eight, nine, ten . . . now I am one, two, three, four!"

My boyfriend and I looked at each other with wide eyes and small smiles. I asked his daughter if she remembered where she lived before, and she pointed out the window in the direction of north and said, "That way!"

I have always believed little ones. Do we really take the time as adults to stop, listen, and learn from them? We should do this more, and play and have fun today. We're only on this fun rock for a short amount of time.

— **MILLIE BLUHM SMITH***

When my son was three, he used to talk about his "other" mother. Out of the blue, he would say that he missed his other mother, and you could physically see and feel his sadness. He'd say, "I had to look after her because my dad died." I asked him if he remembered how his dad died, and he said he was in the Army and was killed in a war. Then, according to my son, when he was older, he joined the Army himself and was killed as well. My son spoke about this several times that year and then just gently forgot.

— **PARE TUTU**
Victoria, Australia

When our son was just beginning to speak, he would point upward and say, "Mommy Daddy." As he grew, my husband and I began to realize his innocent spirituality (we were young, too). When he started to speak in sentences, he'd tell us, "I had a dog like that!" We asked him, "When was that?" He pointed toward a part of the city and said, "When I lived over there," and proceeded to tell us about his life, which sounded very sad, almost lonely.

Soon after this, our son saw the sheets someone had given us for rags, which had black-and-white stripes. He said, "I used to wear that." My husband and I looked at each other and laughed that we had an ex-con living with us!

— **MARIA PALERMO LOCASTRO**
Milton, New York

My wife and I had fraternal twins in 1997. From the time she could speak, our daughter Ashley called my wife's mother "Baka." No one in our family had ever used such a word as a reference toward another person. My mother was referred to by her grandkids as "Nana," and that's what Ashley called her. But she was so insistent and persistent in calling my mother-in-law "Baka" that the name stuck.

We had never even heard the word/name used before by anyone else, so we assumed that this name was unique to our family. Yet a few years later, when our daughters were in preschool, my wife was shocked to overhear one of their classmates call her grandmother "Baka." She asked the other woman about it, and to my wife's surprise, the woman said that *baka* is Croatian for "grandmother"! You can imagine how flabbergasted she was to hear that. All along we thought the name was meaningless, so to find out that it actually meant something in another language floored us! I was a bit skeptical when I first heard this, but I was able to confirm it via the Internet.

We never asked Ashley about it when she was little, so we don't know if my mother-in-law is some past-life Croatian grandmother of hers or Croation is a language familiar to her from a past life . . . whatever the case, it's amazing!

— **JOHN BENSON**
Deerfield, Illinois

When my son, Kris, was around the age of three, we were in the car and I asked him if he would like to go to the bakery for a black-and-white pastry.

He responded, "I don't like black-and-white pastries."

I asked him how he would know that, given that he had never had one before. He said that he had, and then began to cry and told me that he had one with his other mother and father. I asked him, "Which mother and father?" and he said, "You know, my other mother and father, the ones who died in the car accident."

I could only console him and tell him that everything was okay now.

— **NANCY MAHON**
Holtsville, New York

When I was a young child, my family spent a few summers on a lake in the countryside of New Jersey. I was about four or five years old, and I would go down to the grassy area by the lake where many ducks gathered to rest. I would stand on a rock in front of all the ducks and hold an entire Catholic Mass in Latin for them! I was never taught the language and have no idea how I could have done this. I vaguely remember standing before the ducks and having Mass for them, but I do not have any recollection of speaking entirely in Latin. My mother told me that I did this, though, and my sister confirmed it.

— **MARYELLEN COVAIS**
West Melborne, Florida

I have friends who must have had a past-life flashback when they met for the "first time" (in this life). They were only four years old, and the boy knelt down and bowed before the girl. They both started speaking in Chinese for a few minutes, then began to play like nothing happened! The Australian parents of both children, who only spoke English, were speechless for quite a while.

— **ANGELA CHRISTINE JASMINE**
Bargara, Australia

❧ The subject of reincarnation is loaded with controversy, and in some cases, religious taboo strictly prohibits even contemplating it. Yet once again, I encourage you to have a mind that is open to everything and attached to nothing.

I must admit that for a large portion of my own life, my attitude toward past lives and reincarnation was highly skeptical. I then opened up my mind to the idea that in an infinite universe, "all things are possible," and I accepted an invitation to experience a past-life regression firsthand, which I wrote about in depth in a recent book titled *Wishes Fulfilled*. (This session was conducted by Mira Kelley, and I encourage you to read her book, *Beyond Past Lives*.) To this day I can recall every detail of that incredible afternoon, where astounding new insights about past lives were made available to me in 3-D.

I also urge you to take a look at an astonishing book called *Soul Survivor,* about a young boy named James Leininger who was able to give extremely specific information about his previous life as a man named James Huston, a World War II fighter pilot who was shot down on the island of Iwo Jima by the Japanese in that historic battle. At the age of two, James was able to remember and verbalize precise past-life details that have blown away the skeptics who are certain that reincarnation is a fanciful idea but lacks concrete proof.

Soul Survivor was written with meticulous attention to detail by the parents of young James. These parents were so struck by what their little boy was revealing that they even uncovered previously classified information about Iwo Jima, and they actually made contact with the survivors of that battle who knew James Huston personally. Many reviewers of this amazing story have concluded that this is absolute proof of the idea that past lives are an authentic phenomenon.

I implore you to examine the enormous amount of literature now available on the subject of reincarnation, and to make an effort to experience a past-life regression personally, before writing this idea off as New Age blathering. In particular, I beseech you to examine the work of my friend and colleague Brian Weiss, M.D., a graduate of Columbia University and Yale School of Medicine and the author of the classic *Many Lives, Many Masters.* Brian has made the study of past lives the major focus of his venerable career, and the things he discovered in his practice about his patients' recollections while under hypnosis could not be attributable to anything other than the realization of a connection to a past life.

3

MEMORIES OF
CHOOSING PARENTS

❧ I recall a humorous conversation I had with one of my daughters when she was seven years old. Serena was the child who persistently observed my parenting behavior, and was quite frequently very vocal about expressing her displeasure whenever my actions did not meet with her approval. On this particular day, I stopped her from complaining about me and said, "I'm doing the best job I know how to do as your father. If you don't like the way I'm parenting you, I suggest that you stop whining about me, and instead take full responsibility for my actions yourself. You are the one who chose me to be your father, and if you think I'm inadequate in this role, you should be blaming yourself for the bad choice that you made."

She looked at me quite quizzically and replied, "You mean to tell me that I actually picked you to be my father, and Mom to be my mother?" When I told her that was the case, she put her hands on her hips and said, "I must have been in a hurry."

I've always loved this story, and although I was being a bit facetious at the time, in the ensuing years I have come to regard that conversation as having a whole lot more validity than I once could even imagine.

The literature on past-life research seems to support this idea that there actually is a selection process, often in cooperation with "God," in deciding who will be the parents for this baby newly arriving from the world of Spirit. In addition, Dee and I received thousands of responses to our request for parents to give us examples on this topic, and the brief vignettes offered in this chapter are only a small percentage of those we received.

These selections are all the direct record of youngsters, totally unprovoked, spontaneously blurting out words such as, "I am so glad that I picked you to be my mother." Children offer highly specific details about the entire process of picking their parents, very often in cooperation with a God Whom they tend to define as a loving, happy presence. After reviewing the many thousands of responses to our request for stories about life before life, it is impossible not to wonder about this seemingly uncanny phenomenon related by so many people around the world.

Both my wife, Marcelene, and I have always felt that our youngest child, Saje, played a role in bringing her conception to fruition. Something inexplicable took place that night in Brisbane, Australia, back in 1989: An energy awakened my wife and had her acting in ways that she had never before, or since, exhibited in all the years that we were together. It was like a presence saying to both of us, "I've picked you be to to be my parents. Now here I am, tapping on your shoulders and insisting that you cooperate with me and punch my ticket to the Earthbound Express, which will bring me to the life that awaits me with both of you."

When my wife and I returned to the United States and discovered that we had conceived a child that night, both of us knew that something supernatural had taken place, and that our very arrival and presence here on Earth is in the hands of an intelligence that is beyond our human abilities to comprehend it.

I was so profoundly touched by this awareness that I wrote a short poem for my wife, which I titled "Brisbane":

Brisbane
Where God was revealed to us.

Only the two of us know the magic and awe
of that presence.

Against impossible odds . . .

Our connection to eternity further reinforced,
strengthened.

Yet the paradox always lingers . . .

*We are in control/we are not in control,
doomed to make choices.*

*All I am certain of is our love imbedded in
forever.*

So many people report these kinds of interactions with young children who are just beginning to speak. Once again, this is a reminder to have a mind that is open to an idea that seems beyond the realm of possibility to your human mind—but when you consider the concept of an infinite universe supported by a Divine consciousness in which "all things are possible," then perhaps you are living with people who selected you to be their partners on this voyage . . . and you too were once a formless spirit who picked the parents that you would need this time around.

It's all so very fascinating. Enjoy these many stories that innocently came out of the mouths of little ones, who can only speak the truths that they feel.

My five-year-old son, Mather, has beautiful memories of heaven and his time with God.

Our first true-blue conversation on the subject started on a car drive through the country on a beautiful puffy-white-clouds-in-the-sky kind of day. He was completely engrossed in a video game in the backseat while I listened to the radio. About a half hour into the drive, he put his game down and asked, "Mom, do you see that cloud right there?"

I thought he was trying to identify the shapes of the clouds, so I answered him with something silly like, "The one that looks like a mouse?" He said, "No, Mom! That pretty one!" He paused for a while, and then continued, "Well . . . when I was zero, before I was born, I stood on a cloud like that with God." Though I was stunned, I stayed pretty calm and asked him what he was doing on that cloud with God. He said, "We were having fun." He went directly back to his game and wouldn't answer any more questions. I didn't want to pressure him, so I let it rest.

A few weeks later, my husband and I were sitting in the family room. Mather came in, leaned against the wall, and said, "Mom, when I was zero, before I was born, I was standing on the cloud with God. He told me to pick." I asked what God wanted him to pick, and he replied, "He told me to pick my mommy." I said, "Well, buddy, I thank God every day that you picked me to be your mommy." He smiled and said, "When God told me to pick, I looked down and saw mommies everywhere. They all wanted me to pick them, and they were reaching for me. Then I saw you. You were alone and sad and you couldn't find your little boy, and I knew! I knew I loved you and you loved me, so I told God that I wanted you. Mom, when I was zero, before I was born, I picked you."

Through my tears I again thanked him for picking me, and he ran down the hall back to his room. What makes this even more special is that I adopted Mather when he was just a few hours old, and the circumstances of his adoption were and are considered a miracle and a gift by my entire family. I was single and alone at the time, and my first son had passed away 14 years prior (Mather knew nothing of this).

Even though his memories aren't as sharp as they were even six months ago, we've continued to have many conversations about the little things he remembers. I always know when he's going to talk to me about heaven and God because he'll abruptly stop whatever he's doing, look up, and begin, "When I was zero, before I was born . . ." He is an extraordinary child and the love of my life.

— **TINA MITCHELL**
Blackpool, United Kingdom

One night I was sitting on my couch rocking my colicky infant son, PJ, with my three-year-old daughter, Angelica, next to me. I was getting a little frustrated with PJ because he never slept. My daughter said, "Mom, you need to be patient with us because we picked you in heaven." She went on to explain that she sat up in heaven and decided with God whom she should pick as a mom and dad—she waited until she could pick the perfect ones. When she saw her dad and me, she told God that she was ready to go. Angelica said that her brother had done the same thing, so I needed to be patient with him.

Wow! Everything I did as a parent and as a person changed at that moment. As a profession, I teach multiple handicapped students, and I realize that patience and tolerance and kindness are the most important gifts that I can give while I am on this earth.

— **SHEILA PINO MUSSA**
Northfield, New Jersey

When my daughter was about three years old, she mentioned in a conversation that she liked it when she was in heaven! I was a little sad that day because she had told me that she wished her daddy was home with us, like other children (we got divorced when she was a newborn). Then she said, "But that's okay, because I knew it would be like this."

I asked her what she meant by that, and she answered, "Mommy, when I was in heaven, I picked you. And I knew we were going to be alone, so that's okay. Don't worry, Mommy, I love you so much." That was so amazing for me to hear.

— **ELSIE FARFAN**
Henderson, Nevada

When my daughter was born in August 2006, I knew she was someone special, but I felt that I wasn't her mom. It was weird because she came from my womb, so why was I having this feeling?

When Alannah was about three, she came up to me one day and said, "Mommy, can I tell you something?" I said, "Yes, you can tell me anything." Then she told me something that shocked me. She said, "Mommy, when I was looking to come here, I was looking for Nani [my mother], but I couldn't find her. I searched for her and still couldn't find her. I really wanted her to be my mommy, but I found you and then I chose you. Mommy, we are supposed to be sisters, did you know?"

I reflected back on that feeling of not being her mom, and my mouth dropped open. Wow! I didn't know how to respond to this at first, but then after a minute, I asked, "So we're sisters?" She said, "Well, not right now anymore, but that's why I was looking for Nani, so we could be sisters again." This explained why I'd had that feeling before.

Alannah proceeded to tell me how God is a great big God, He is very nice, and He is something we need in our lives to be completely happy and whole. She has always had a strong connection to God, and I have to say it is a privilege to take care of one of His little Earth angels.

— **ARLENE MORA**
Spring Valley, California

My son, Noah, who is now six years old, has been intuitive from the moment he entered this lifetime. He knows all about his chakras and spirit guides, and talks quietly in his room to his spirit guide "Bill" often. I even have a video of him playing while orbs were dancing all around him!

Noah often puts his hands on my head, arm, or stomach when I'm not feeling well, and within minutes I feel 100 percent better. He is a beautiful, bright, shining light, and I am blessed to be his mommy! He is my greatest teacher.

A couple of years ago, I asked him, "Noah, what are angels like?"

"Mommy, you know!"

I replied, "No, I forget because I'm older! You're young—you just came from there—so I'd really like to know!"

Without pausing he said, "They are sometimes purple, sometimes all colors, and big and bright. They love lots. I play with the angels lots. When you were ready for me, the angels cried because they were sad I was leaving them. They only cry when their babies go, but they were happy we picked you!"

My little four-year-old, with wisdom in his eyes deeper than any ocean on this earth, truly moved me. I teared up, hugged him, and said, "I'm so happy you picked me, too!"

— **STEPHANIE VAN DE VEN**
Ayr, Ontario, Canada

I am 73 years old, and this incident has been a part of my life since I was about 3.

I remember telling my parents that I had chosen them before I was born. They simply patted me on the head and smiled at what they considered to be the imaginings of a young child. Not so! I remember this as clearly today as I did then. I told them that I was somewhere up above the earth looking down at a gathering of several pairs of people. I then heard a voice ask me which ones I wanted as my parents. I was told that whichever couple I chose would teach me what I needed to learn in this lifetime. I pointed to my parents and replied, "I'll take them."

— JUDY SMITH*

One night at dinner, our younger foster/adopted son (he was around four years old) started talking at great length about his life "in the stars" and how he had all these brothers and sisters who lived there. He said he'd seen my husband and me from there and tried to get our attention many times but we never could see him, so he decided to be born through his mom so we could find him.

My husband and I were floored to say the least. I'd had a few miscarriages after my first son, so once my younger son told us what he'd seen, I knew his soul had been trying to come in through me even though my body was not able to do it. We feel our older son always knew the plan because he was the one constantly begging us for a sibling. Once his brother came to live with us (placed with us at 22 months old), he was so happy to have him here even though it wasn't easy in the beginning. They are now the best of friends.

— **MELISSA HELD-WEGNER**
Longmont, Colorado

I am a teacher of special-needs kids (we refer to many of them as Indigos). One of the children was able to recall being born, conversations between the midwife and his mother during birth, the noises his mother made, the names of those in the room during his birth, and so on. Finding that interesting, when I got home that night, I asked my son if he himself remembered being born. What follows is our conversation on the subject.

Me: Hey, Kaelan, do you remember being born? Like when you came out of my tummy in the hospital?

Kaelan: Um . . . no. But I do remember just after when you were holding me. I was very happy and I smiled.

Me: Why were you so happy?

Kaelan: Because you were the one that I picked.

Me: What do you mean, "The one that I picked"?

Kaelan: Well, you know, like when you're in heaven, and you're picking out who you want to be your mommy?

Me (very surprised and taken aback): No, honey, I don't, but please tell me what you remember.

Kaelan: Well, you were the mommy I picked and that made me happy.

Me: Why did you pick me?

Kaelan: Because I knew you were going to be nice and help me. I didn't have nice moms very much many times. Oh, and you were funny.

Me (trying to choke back tears): Oh! That is so nice! I'm glad you picked me!

Kaelan: Yeah, but . . . you're not as funny as I thought you'd be.

Me (after stifling a bit of laughter and the feeling of being a wee bit insulted): How did you know that I would be a good mom and help you?

Kaelan: Because you had a high number above your head.

Me: What do you mean by "a high number"?

Kaelan: You had a big number, like floating above your head. If the number was the biggest of the other ones, then I knew that would be the best mom to pick.

Me (still not quite understanding the number significance, but wanting to keep him talking before he ran off): Well, what am I supposed to help you with? What are you supposed to learn?

Kaelan: I already know lots of things; I just can't remember them.

Me: But what is Mommy supposed to help you with? What do you think you are here in this life to learn?

Kaelan: Oh, to be nice and love people this time.

— **JANNA SIMMERSON**
Alberta, Canada

My daughter was born in 1969. When she was three, we were sitting at the table having lunch and out of the blue she said, "I picked you and Daddy out of a bunch of other mommies and daddies." This caught my attention, so I said, "What? How did you do this?" Her reply was, "There was a long line of mommies and daddies, and I went down the line. When I saw you, I knew you were mine." And then she was off to something that had happened earlier in the day. She never chose to offer any more on the subject beyond that, and I did ask her a few other times.

— **LINDA JONES**
Lolo, Montana

My daughter tells me all the time that she came to me from the stars, that she chose my husband and me to be her mommy and daddy while she was in the stars. And that she has three daughters who are in the stars but will one day come down to be her children.

— **LARA KRETLER**
Lewis Center, Ohio

Our son, Benjamin Forrest Barker, was born on July 19, 1993, and passed away on June 30, 2014. He was a very strong-willed child from the day of his conception. After I had a twin ectopic pregnancy, I was told by fertility experts that it was highly unlikely that I would be able to conceive a child naturally due to the damage in my fallopian tubes. Upon Benjamin's birth, it was determined that he swam in and out of the hole in my damaged tubes toward my uterus for implantation. At three months' gestation, I felt him move and kick, but the doctor said that was unlikely. When I was several months along, the doctor noticed bruises on my stomach, which was extremely unusual—my son was so active and strong that he'd bruised me from the inside out.

Benjamin spoke very well from a young age. For example, when he was about two and a half, he would repeatedly tell me that he remembered being in my belly and what it was like. When he would say that he didn't want to come out, I would think of his long birth via C-section—our doctor had joked that the baby was holding on to my ribs and heart and didn't want out. The doctor said he'd never seen anything like that.

When Benjamin was around three, one day he told me that he "chose" his dad and me, and over the next few years, he continued to tell my husband and me that he wanted us to be his parents and had chosen us. It was so surprising but very loving and sweet for our baby to tell us that.

Our son passed away unexpectedly. He was very spirited and intuitive, and our gift from God. He was only here for a short time and touched many lives, a true angel.

— **KATHLEEN BARKER***

I have two children: a boy named Lucas, who is eight; and a daughter named Sara, who is four. When Lucas was four and a half, he had a hard time sleeping. As an exhausted pregnant woman whose husband works until midnight, I had to make the decision to let Lucas sleep with me one evening.

While we were lying in bed, my son placed his hand on my stomach and said, "Do you know how long I've waited for you to be my mom?" I replied, "No, how long?" He said, "A long, long time. I picked you to be my mom because I love you so much." Lucus repeatedly went back to the point of how long the wait was.

— **CHRIS SAWMILLER**
Wyandotte, Michigan

I have discovered that when I need to learn something, it keeps showing up in my life. I heard that we "choose our parents," so I talked about this with my boss, Laura, whom I've known for more than six years and have had countless enlightening conversations with. She has told me many stories of her son, whom she had after ten years of trying to have a baby.

I said, "Laura, I keep hearing that we choose our parents." She immediately started tearing up and said, "Oh, that means Anthony picked me!" She was so touched.

That very next morning, Laura called me into her office and asked me to close the door. She told me that the night before, as she was putting her son to bed, she kept hugging and kissing him and telling him, "Oh, Anthony, I love you. Do you know how much Mommy and Daddy love you? We love you so much." Finally, Anthony shook off her hugs and kisses and said, "I know! I know, Mommy, that's why I chose you!"

"What do you mean?!"

"Yes, Spirit showed me three families [holding up three fingers to denote the families] and now, I know it was the Holy Spirit. I saw that you and Daddy really wanted a baby and that's why I chose you."

"And who were the other families?" She tried to interrogate him further.

Anthony put his hands over his ears and shook his head. "I don't remember, I don't remember!"

When Laura told me this, an electric shiver went up and down my body. I knew that it was true: We do choose our parents, and little Anthony remembered.

— **BRIGITTE COTA**
Cerritos, California

When my daughter was about three, she told me that mine was not the first belly she came to—but the other mom had too many kids already, so she didn't stay there.

— **CHERYL A. BONESTEEL**
Center Valley, Pennsylvania

My son was around age four when we were playing our game of "I love you more because . . ."

I told him, "I love you more because . . . I love you beyond infinity, around the moon two times, around Mars, and touching every star on the way back to you." Pretty great answer, right? I had him beat. Or at least I thought I did.

Very seriously, my son placed his hands on either side of my face, locked his crystal blue eyes with mine, and said, "Mommy! I love you more because I picked you while I was in heaven."

Needless to say, he won the game.

— **SHARI RIGHTMER**
Taft, California

When my son was just shy of three, I was carrying him up to bed. He was in a happy, relaxed stare, and out of the blue said, "When I was in heaven, the earth looked different . . . He understood me and realized I wanted to come back down into your belly."

I asked him, "Are you talking about God?"

"Yes, I was with God, but I don't remember what He was like now."

"And you told him you wanted to come back down in my belly?!"

He said, "No, I didn't tell him, He understood me."

I'd had a miscarriage before him, and had never talked about it with him.

— **SHANNON DESILETS**
Pembroke, New Hampshire

When my son was very small, he began talking early, with a well-rounded vocabulary and great pronunciation. My husband and I did not really teach our children about God even though I am a firm believer. Our son was just too small to grasp it, or so we thought.

While sitting and playing with his toys one day, my son looked at me and, out of nowhere, said, "Did you know that God lets us choose our parents while in heaven, and I picked you?"

The look on his face was so full of purpose and love, not like a small child's joke. It has made a huge impact on me and will always stay in my mind. That was 17 years ago.

— **JESSICA MAGGARD**
Satellite Beach, Florida

At the age of five, my younger son announced out of the blue that he had chosen my wife and me to be his parents. Intrigued, my wife asked how he had done this. He matter-of-factly stated that while he was in heaven before he was born, he had been allowed to go through one door to pick his parents, and through another door to select his brothers and sisters. We were not churchgoers, and have no knowledge of his having obtained this idea from any external source.

— **ROBERT J. RINNE**
Orthez, France

My youngest son, Christopher, is now 20. I believe he must have been about three or so when he was sitting on my lap in the rocker in his room, and we were reading stories. He turned to me and said, "I'm glad I picked you." I asked him what he meant, and he told me that he was up in heaven with God, and God took him to a certain spot to look down at all the parents and asked Christopher to pick out his mommy and daddy. I was so startled I didn't ask any more questions.

— **ELAINE PONICHTERA**
Depew, New York

My three-year-old told me that when she was in heaven with God, she picked me as her mother because God assured her that she would be happy and loved by me and the rest of the family. She is and will be my only child, so she got that right!

— **NORAIMA PADILLA**
Riverdale, New York

When I wrote my first book four years ago, in the Acknowledgments, I thanked my son and daughter for "choosing" me to be their mom. I just had a deep feeling that it was true. Then about a year later, I was having a conversation with my 23-year-old daughter about the whole concept of spirits entering this world.

I told her that I believe we choose the experiences we want to have, as well as how we enter this world and through whom.

She didn't miss a beat when she said, "Mom, remember when I was about three years old and I told you I chose you to be my mommy?" I froze—I hadn't remembered until she said that, but she never forgot!

Also, when my son was two years old, he was in the backyard riding his bike, and I was sitting at the kitchen table. The back door was open so I could easily see him—the yard was fenced in, and he was scooting along having a good time. I didn't hear him anymore, so I looked out into the yard to see what he was doing. He was just sitting there. Something had captured his attention; he was fixated on something and then started waving.

I was very curious as to what he was looking and waving at, so I got up and went to him. I asked what he was looking at, and he said "Pop-Pop!" Immediately my body filled with goose bumps. I said, "You can see Pop-Pop?" He said emphatically, "Yes! Pop-Pop is in the sky! He's going away for a long time, Mommy, but I will see him again."

I love this stuff!

— **LISA M. SAUNDERS**
Randallstown, Maryland

When my son was the ripe old age of three, he had drawn this beautiful tree while playing alone in his room. I was an at-home mom, and he hadn't been to any form of preschool. Astonished, I asked, "Marley, where did you learn to draw such a beautiful tree?" His response was, "Mama, God taught me when I was in heaven." We didn't belong to a church or read from the Bible; we talked of God but not a lot. I was so shocked by his response, but my heart swelled!

Another time when he was about the same age, out of the blue, he started talking of how he remembered looking down at his dad and me from heaven with God and chose us as his parents. How beautiful!

— **SHERRI BRANCH GORAL**
Minnetonka, Minnesota

My son Matthew is a twin. When he was four, I asked him what his earliest memory was. He proceeded to describe a moment when he was sitting up above the clouds with God, and he looked down and chose me to be his mother. I was surprised at the time—I hadn't been aware of anyone discussing the notion that we choose our parents. I asked Matthew why he chose me, and he shyly replied, "You looked nice."

It wasn't until a couple of years later, when I was watching Oprah interview Brian Weiss and he explained that we chose our parents, that I truly understood what my son had been telling me.

— **MEROPI DIMOTAKIS**
Victoria, Australia

I had a termination while receiving a treatment for a back problem, and it broke my heart. Years later my back healed and I had a beautiful baby girl. When she was two, she was sitting there with a book and just looked up at me and said, "Mummy, you sent me back the first time because you had a bad back, but I came back when your back was better."

— **MARIE BIRKETT**
Southampton, United Kingdom

My son constantly talks about how excited he was as a baby in my belly, waiting for me; how scared he was to come out; and how happy he was to finally see my face. I always thought he was being creative.

He had hearing problems as a child, which were remedied with a surgery. When he came out of the anesthesia, I sang to him. He grabbed my face, eyes wide, and said, "Mommy! Your voice is so beautiful! This was the voice I chose!" Again, I thought he was just telling stories. Hearing other people share their experiences makes me think there was more going on than I thought, though.

— **ERIN MICHELLE THRELFALL**
Brooklyn, New York

One day I told my daughter, "If God would have allowed me to pick any little girl in this whole wide world, I would have picked you." Every time she sees our wedding picture she says, "Diosito [God] let me peek down from heaven and see you get married. He told me, 'Those are your parents.'" She said she was allowed to see this and "two other little angels." We only have two children, so one more must be waiting to join our family.

— **LETICIA DUGGAN**
Los Angeles, California

My son spoke very early. When he was under the age of 2 (he's now 14), we were sitting on the bed relaxing and cuddling, and he told me how he was happy because he picked me to be his momma and my husband to be his daddy. I asked how he picked us, and he said that God helped him. I asked how, and he said that God hugged him and helped him go down, down, down into my tummy, and he stayed there until it was time to be born. Then he "got born," and he was so happy because I was there and Daddy was there, and it was "boo-i-ful."

— **MICHELLE MOORE-FREEMAN***

When my son was two or three, he told me with great confidence, "Before I was in your tummy, I told God that I picked you to be my mommy. I'm so glad I did."

— **CARLA HELMBRECHT**
San Francisco, California

Sebastian was about three or four years old when he first told me, "You know, when I was in heaven I chose you to be my mom." It brought tears to my eyes because I felt it was true. I replied, "I am so happy you chose me, because I asked God during a whole year to send me a son." He said, "I know. God told me, then I decided you will be my mom."

— **VIVIANA CARTER**
Concepción, Chile

When my second son was born, he always seemed to prefer his dad to me, and I realized that my feelings while pregnant with him may have had something to do with that. I wasn't ready to be pregnant again, but my husband and firstborn son both wanted another "now," so I reluctantly agreed.

One day when my youngest was about six, I explained that to him and added, "But, honey, if I knew it was going to be *you,* I would have had you in a heartbeat!" He jumped up and wrapped his arms around my neck and cried, "Oh, Mommy! If only you knew how *long* I waited up there for you!"

From that point on, all of his resistance toward me completely vanished.

— **JILL LAMBERT**
Conway, Arizona

As a toddler, my daughter, Nanci, always seemed to be more enlightened than many of the adults around her. She often removed herself from negative situations by simply walking away, and she saw the good in everything. One day I asked her if she remembered anything from a time before she came to our world. She replied, "Yes, I remember sitting with God. We picked you together. I am your present."

Just telling this story all these years later (18 at least) brings a tear to my eye and a lump to my throat. No truer words were ever spoken—Nanci is the greatest gift I have ever had the privilege to receive.

— **LENORE DILIEGRO**
Revere, Massachusetts

✍ Assume for just one moment—with a mind that is open to all things being possible in an infinite universe—that the premise of this chapter is undeniably true. That is, that in a very mysterious way not understood by our human minds, we are all somehow involved in selecting our parents for this earthbound journey called our life. Now, if you are a parent, ask yourself, *Why would each of my children have chosen me to be one of their parents? And am I fulfilling this chosen role to the very best of my ability?*

Have a conversation with your children and ask them why they would have chosen you if they had that opportunity even before they were born. These kinds of questions can stimulate fascinating and compelling discussions that could lead to improving your relationship with your children, regardless of their current age. If you are the parent of a toddler, I encourage you to be open to anything that your child might say, particularly if they offer any clues that they remember being on the parental-selection committee while still residing exclusively in the world of Spirit.

I would encourage you to examine what possible motive you might have had in picking your own parents as well. At one time in my life I couldn't have imagined why I would had picked my own father, a man who abandoned me as an infant, and who was an irresponsible drunkard who spent a great deal of time chasing women, stealing, and being incarcerated. I spent a great deal of my life searching for this man with a heart filled with anger and even rage.

However, it was at his gravesite ten years after his passing that I began to understand why I ultimately came to address my father as "my greatest teacher." It was in forgiving him and overcoming my inner fury that I was able to align with my true calling. Perhaps, just perhaps, I picked my father in order to experience the healing power of love, and to become a teacher of higher consciousness, which includes forgiveness as a major tenet.

MEMORIES OF FAMILY REINCARNATIONS AND ROLE REVERSALS

∽ The subject of reincarnation taking place within the same family over many generations was a common theme in the responses we received from people all over the world. It seems that young children have very specific memories of having lived in a previous lifetime as someone within their current family. This idea of "family return" demonstrates precisely how incredibly personal reincarnation can be, and that emotional and relationship issues can persist from one lifetime to the next. In fact, this idea of reincarnation taking place over and over within the same family is so pervasive in the literature on past lives that an entire book has been written on the subject—*Return from Heaven* by Carol Bowman offers thousands upon thousands of examples of this phenomenon.

There are many instances of a soul apparently making amends to another soul within the family by returning again as a child. I call these "role reversals," and many such illustrations are offered here in this fourth chapter. Dee and I received hundreds of stories in which astounded parents were told: "I used to be your mommy, now you're mine," or "Remember when you were a baby and I used to feed you?" These kinds of sentiments when spoken by children who are very serious about what they're saying often produce an incredulous response from the older and "wiser" adults. Most often, little ones simply state what they feel as a fact. They are not interested in proving a point or winning an argument about the veracity of past-life theory; they're just expressing what they know to be true for them.

Some people remember their dreams, while others do not. Similarly, it seems that some people remember their past lives, while others have absolutely no recollection of anything of this nature. A baby who is born into a family can be the soul of a loved one who died, and there seems to be a preponderance of evidence to support such a conclusion. What you will see here in this chapter is a large body of anecdotal evidence to at least allow you to have an open mind about such a possibility.

This is not to say that every single baby born into a family is a reincarnated ancestor; however, after examining a mountain of evidence, much of it offered by highly credentialed scholars who have studied this subject in depth, I have opened my mind to this reality. We do not profess to know the reasons for one soul to return to a family after many generations, but there are enough people here on our planet who report such narratives over and over again that I encourage you to look at your tiny children and wonder who they were before they showed up here in your family. That could be Grandpa you're cuddling and feeding with a bottle. Isn't that delicious to contemplate?

I have a four-year-old son whose name is Noah. He never knew his grandfather (my father), as he passed away in 2002. About a year ago, we were spending an afternoon together. At some point completely out of the blue, as we were walking up the stairs, he turned around and said, "You know, Daddy, when you were my age, I was your daddy!"

The first thought that crossed my mind was, *Could he actually be my father's reincarnation?* Then I asked, "How do you know that?" To which he simply responded, "I know," and then moved on to continue his activity.

— **DIDIER BRUN**
Dubai, United Arab Emirates

My mom was pregnant and lost the baby, who was going to be named Nicole. About two years later I became pregnant and decided to name my baby Nicole. Mom and I talked about the possibility that it was the same soul who'd tried to come through her.

When Nicole was about five years old, she said, "Mommy, before I was in your tummy, I was in Gammie's tummy." I burst into tears, and of course called my mom right away to tell her what Nicole had just said. That was our confirmation.

— **JODY STRUCK AMSBERRY***

When my granddaughter, Elise, was about two years old, I remarked to her how she reminded me of my grandmother, who had partially raised me and passed away about 50 years ago. Elise said, "I know, because I am her." At that young age, she wasn't joking or trying to put me on . . . she was merely stating what was true for her. Her statement was so profound. I will never forget it.

— JACQUELINE JEWETT
Santa Rosa, California

I wrote about this story in my book *Breath of a Child*. I can remember being two years old and having lunch with my mother, when I looked at her and felt to the depths of my soul what I said to her: "I used to be your mommy; now you're mine." I never forgot it but kept it to myself.

Years later, my own daughter turned to me one afternoon and said, "I used to be your mommy, and now you're mine." That was so profound for me, and

I knew the feeling I had as a child was confirmed. If you think about it, we were in reverse in another life.

— **DONNA RINELLI**
Edgewater, Florida

My grandson, Louis-David, was about four or five years old when he began mentioning memories of my father, whom he had never met, smiling with the very same special gleam in his eye when he did things similar to how my dad had done them. One day, he said to me, "I remember being him . . . I remember you." We had no movies or specific pictures; we often spoke of Grandma, but rarely Grandpa.

To this day, even though I have no proof of past lives, I still wonder. My dad went to war and it totally destroyed him. Louis was born flat-footed—I suppose if he is my dad, he sure did not want to go to war again. My dad had one arm partially bent at the elbow (I never knew why)—Louis fell and broke his arm, and now his arm moves in the same partially bent way. There are many other things like those examples. I am not saying I believe this or that; I'm just stating observations.

— **SYLVIE PERRAS**
Laval, Quebec, Canada

I have four children, but only came into my deep spiritual awareness when my youngest, Raphael, was born. I so wish I'd been more awakened with my other three—I can't imagine the fun things I dismissed or just plain didn't hear.

One evening when Raphael was about two, we were lying in bed reading, and out of the blue he said, "Do you remember when I had that other mommy?" Thankfully, I had recently seen Brian Weiss on *Oprah*, so it didn't totally shock me! I told him, "No, I don't . . . what else do you remember?" And he said, "I don't know. But then do you remember that other time when I was the mommy and you were the kid?" I was just, like, *Wow, this is incredible to witness.* I said, "No, I wish I remembered. Was is pretty cool?" He said, "Yes, but I like this a lot, too."

It was amaze-bombs to have that happen!

— **COLETTE LONGIN**
Great Falls, Montana

One day when my daughter, Rebecca, was three, we were playing in her room and she asked, "Do you remember when I was your mommy?"

"No, tell me about that," I said, with chills running through me.

"I wasn't very nice to you. Do you remember?"

"No, I don't remember anymore."

"Well, I'm glad you're my mommy now."

Now Rebecca is 13 and has no recollection of this exchange. I wish I had known what to do to keep her connected to this knowing.

— **SUSAN KOENIG**
Centereach, New York

I asked my granddaughter when she was three if we had ever been together before she came here. She said, "Yes, I was your mumma!" It sent chills all over my body, and I knew it was true.

— **TERESA JACKSON**
New Gloucester, Maine

Years ago when my daughter was not quite three, I was working the night shift as a registered nurse and would spend my days dozing on the couch in order to "keep an eye on her." She was always a solicitous little one, and would come by and stroke my head as I napped. One particular day as she patted my head and face, she said (and I will remember this always), "Don't you remember? I used to be your mother."

That woke me up! I must have looked surprised, because then she repeated the same thing. I told my husband, and we were both open to the idea that she may have memories of that time in between. As the years progressed, I often asked her if she remembered telling me that, and of course as she got older, she'd laugh and say, "Yes, and don't you forget it!"

— **SUZANNE ROBINSON**
Seminole, Florida

At the age of two, my son told me, "I am your father and son." He was born the same day that my father passed away.

— **HANS GROENLAND***

When my daughter was three or four, she was frustrated after I'd scolded her for something. She put her hands on her hips, stared me straight in the eye, and said, "Well! It didn't work that way when *I* was *your* mother."

She went on playing, and left me standing there, completely stunned. It could have been a chance comment, but the calm authority with which it was spoken gave me pause.

— **DY CYMRAES**
Westminster, Maryland

My granddaughter, Ellie, has been trying to *seriously* get my attention about her former identity since she was about nine months old. She continually brought me my grandmother's picture of Mary and Jesus, which was an odd choice for a baby just crawling with toys all around! She then wanted to take it home, so I gave it to her.

When Ellie was a year old, she was in the downstairs playroom and, out of the 27 books down there, picked one that my grandmother had given me, called *The Chinese Children Next Door* by Pearl Buck. I did not know I had this book! Several months later, she then picked out *Now We Are Six* by A. A. Milne, out of a pile of over 30 books on her big sister's shelf. That was another book given to me by the same grandmother! Her sister told her that she could not have it as it was a very old book. Ellie said, "Mine!" and ran down the hall with it clutched under her arm like a football. We could not get her to release it.

It was at that moment that I realized it in fact really was her book, as she has the soul of my favorite grandmother, who has returned for a new cycle of life! I told Ellie that I finally knew this, and she gave me the hugest smile of relief. At 20 months, she does not call me Grammy like the other grandchildren but Becky, as my grandmother called me "Becky the Specky." It's great because I sing Ellie all of the old songs that my grandmother taught me, and she is in *heaven* when we sing those from the *Hans Christian Andersen* soundtrack.

This all may sound weird, but I am totally thrilled to have her with me again in brand-new ways and feel a remarkable sense of peace.

— **BECKY BRITTAIN, PH.D.**
St. Louis, Missouri

My son was two and playing intently with his toys when he matter-of-factly said, "Remember when you were a baby and I used to feed you?"

He was born a year to the day after my grandpa died. One day, when he was five, he asked me, "What day is it?"

"Thursday," I replied.

"No, like, what date is it?" It was my grandpa's birthday.

— **STACEY KNIGHT-GRIFFITH**
Rochester, Illinois

I met a physician a little while ago (I'll call her "Mary") who told me a very interesting story. Mary's firstborn child died before she was one. Mary used to sing a lullaby that was especially for her baby, and when she died suddenly, Mary never sang that song again. After seven years, Mary had another little girl who began to sing the lullaby at the age of four. Mary froze and asked her daughter how she knew the song. The child's response was, "Mommy, you used to sing it to me."

Mary became a true believer after that, and understood that you pick your mother and father before you are born.

— **ANNA KIELY**
Victoria, Australia

My oldest daughter, Shea, once told me something interesting when she was three years old: "Mom, remember when I was the mom and you were the kid?" Wow! It kinda made me think for a minute, but my response was, "Umm . . . no, honey, I don't."

— **ALICIA BOOTH**
Grand Blanc, Michigan

My son was two when he told me that he used to be my father. Two separate times he said this.

— **LOUISE PARDI MAZZA**
New Hartford, New York

I was visiting my grandsons when Jake was four and Noah was two. As he was munching thoughtfully on his cereal one morning, Jake told me, "In my past life, I died in quicksand and Mama died trying to save me. Noah was my twin and he didn't die, so he was really scared when we were gone. So when we decided to be born again, we chose Mommy and Daddy to be our parents again."

"Where were you when you chose them?" I asked.

He looked upward and exclaimed, "We were up there looking down on Mommy and Daddy! Where else would we be?"

"Well, I was just wondering," I replied.

Then without missing a beat, he continued, "You're all gold like Noah and me. Mama's blue, Daddy's green, and you are gold—but you have a big blue light that comes out of the middle of your forehead."

My daughter, who was working in the kitchen, explained, "He sees auras."

— **CARRIE HUNTER**
Victoria, British Columbia, Canada

My three-year-old daughter told me that she was her grandma Rosie's little boy. I told her, "No, you have always been a little girl." She said, "You don't understand—I was her little boy, and I died when I was almost four." I didn't know enough to follow up with other questions, such as "Where did you live?" and so forth. But almost ten years later I found out that Rosie's son had died at about three years of age, and both children had blue eyes and blonde hair.

My daughter is now 30 and has no memory of any of this.

— **JUDY KNICELY**
Newark, Ohio

When my oldest son, David, was little, we were driving along the Pacific Coast Highway in Cayucos, California, when he began telling of a previous life we had together. In this story, he used vivid and very descriptive words for a four-year-old. He described the clothing of the era, as well as the activity of a large ship crossing an ocean.

He said that we were on this ship and it was sinking: "You remember, right, Mom, the day I drowned on that boat? I told you then you would be my mom again, and here we are driving by the water where I died."

— **TERESA NEWTON-HUGHES**
Newbury Park, California

Before he was two years old, my son assumed a persona I didn't recognize. He was looking at me like I was a stranger and said, "Where's my 'nother mother? She don't look like you. She don't smell like you neither." I asked him what happened to her. He said, "One too many smokes." He was this really tough little character with a different accent and attitude. I'm pretty sure he'd never heard the expression "smokes"—I would have said "cigarettes," and I don't think we even knew anyone who smoked.

Another time at age five, he told my sister, "You know, you've got an old man on your head." She asked, "What does he look like?" He gestured with claw marks down his cheeks and said, "He's really old." My sister said, "That's Pop." It was her father-in-law who had been in a car accident and had scars down his cheeks, and had died some years earlier. It turns out that my niece had also seen and interacted with Pop.

— **KAYE HALL**
Nightcliff, Australia

I am, among other things, the mother of three children—two daughters and one son. I grew up in a strict Christian religion in southwest Virginia and went on to be a hippie chick, so the belief in reincarnation was not something I had even heard about.

On the evening of November 27, 1987, I was involved in a car accident that resulted in the death of my two-and-a-half-year-old son, Nathan. I cannot say with words how dark my world became in that moment, and it stayed that way for several years after, because in that darkness was the only place I thought my son existed anymore.

After a couple of years in the darkness, I reflected back on the day leading up to Nathan's death, as I had done ten million times before. At this point I think something inside of me was hoping for some sense of closure, even though, intellectually, I didn't know what I was looking for. I did need to accept the idea that Nathan was gone and he was never coming back, though.

As I worked at this acceptance and started examining things, I knew without a doubt that that was the day Nathan had chosen to leave his physical body—there were too many "coincidences" to dismiss his death as an "accident." After a time of seeking acceptance, acceptance was found. And I came to see how intricately connected and interdependent everything and every event is.

There is no better reward in this life than having grandchildren. I know grandparents say this all the time, but it is so true. You think you could not possibly love anyone or anything more than your own kids, and then the grandkids come and you just think your heart is surely going to burst with all the love you experience. My eldest daughter had a son, then my youngest had a son soon after, then my eldest had another son then another son, and then nothing—it was as if the well dried up, but I really wanted a granddaughter.

A few years later I moved to a new city, and my youngest daughter came back to West Virginia with her husband and son. It wasn't long after that she announced that she was pregnant. I was ecstatic—I already cherished this baby because I just *knew* it was my granddaughter. That was confirmed on Friday, April 13, 2008, when my Butterfly, little Kayla Bug, came forth into this world and she was just perfect.

I adored and cherished her, but it was not easy for her mother or me—this child cried for a solid year, and nothing we could do would console her. But then Kayla became a happy child and the very light of my existence. We had bonded even while she was in her mommy's tummy, but that bond only grew stronger and stronger with time.

One day I was picking up Kayla and her two brothers for a weekend at Ganny's and Pap Pap's house. My daughter and her husband were moving and needed some time to pack without kids. While I was there, my daughter told me that she'd noticed Kayla watching her take down a baby picture of my son, Nathan. She said to my daughter, "I play with him. He flies." My daughter said that she got the chills, and I must admit I was very moved by this information. Yet what happened next is still a mystery to me.

As I was backing out of the parking space, Kayla announced, "I am a girl."

Noticing the differences between boys and girls had been a new thing with her of late, and so I simply agreed. "Yes, Kayla, you are a girl. Isaiah is a boy, and Blake is a boy."

"I used to be a boy when I was a little baby like Blakey," she quickly informed me. *Okay,* I thought, *let's get to the bottom of this.* I also knew that I had to be very light and jovial with my questions so as not to lead her in any direction. So I replied, "You were? Well, if you were a little boy when you were a baby like Blakey, what was your name when you were a little boy?"

Without hesitation, she chirped back in her three-year-old pronunciation, "Natan." Well, now she had my attention on a whole new level, but I couldn't let it show, not even in the subtlest of ways. However, I still wasn't convinced of anything just yet because she has an older cousin named Nathan, and she just worshipped the ground he walked on. It would only stand to reason that if she imagined being a boy, she would choose her cousin.

With 99 percent confidence in my prediction that she would give me the name of her auntie and my eldest daughter, I asked the next question: "So, when you were a little boy and your name was Nathan, who was your mommy?"

Again the answer came without hesitation. "You were, Ganny," she said, in a tone that conveyed that I was being completely silly to even ask that question.

I have never asked her anything more about the time when she was a little boy named Nathan and I was her mommy; today, she is a little girl named Kayla and I am her Ganny. Although I do prefer her description of who I am to her in this lifetime. While coming home from day care one day, she piped up from the backseat to ask, "Hey, Mommy, do you know what my Ganny is?"

Her mom replied, "No, Kayla, what is your Ganny?"

And the answer she gave will be with me, stamped on my heart and soul, for all of eternity: "She is my Lady Bug." And so it is and ever shall be with the Lady Bug and the Butterfly.

I can't explain how she could play with that little boy in the picture—my son, Nathan—and also embody his soul. I just can't explain that, even with all I now believe about reincarnation. I suppose that is one of those details I will leave to the people who speak in deep voices as they channel the saints and spirit guides. But, then, the Butterflies never need to explain such things to the Lady Bugs.

— **CONNIE NEVILLE-DORFNER, AKA THE LADY BUG**
South Charleston, West Virginia

✎ Whenever you hear a child speak of these great mysteries that have perplexed our most learned scholars from time immemorial, keep in mind that their memories of the spiritual realm are still very fresh and current. Whenever a child shares their memories of being in the same family in a different role, perhaps as a parent or grandparent, know that they are communicating from a mind that is uncontaminated by the ideas and teachings we adults have been indoctrinated with. They are simply speaking their truth. Recall what Jesus said in the scriptures, that we must be like children in order to enter the kingdom of heaven.

I do not profess to understand the reason why so many children recall having been a member of a family in a previous lifetime, but surely it cannot be a huge coincidence that there are literally millions of documented examples of children blurting out these remembrances, in all corners of the globe, and going back as far as antiquity.

I urge you to be as inquisitive with little ones as possible, without appearing to doubt them. Treat their statements as factual, and encourage them to speak freely and openly about their own unique understandings. Ask them questions that encourage them to further explore this incredible idea of family reincarnation. Show them the stories that many other children have reported, including those that appear in these pages, as well as the huge body of research that is available in books and online. Make this an idea that comes alive for them, rather than a subject that you push aside because it might interfere with some long-held notions of the absurdity of such an idea, or because it might conflict with some cultural or religious teaching that you may have unconsciously adopted as an unassailable truth.

Finally, I would beseech you to do some family research when these kinds of reincarnation statements surface from the mouths of very young children. Before the memories fade—and in virtually all cases, this is what happens—encourage the child to be as specific as possible about their memories of a lifetime before they were born. Listen for the sincerity in their voices and look for any factual tidbits that might give you some information to validate what they're offering you with their recollections. You will find that there are frequently details that go way beyond coincidence, which point to the veracity of what they are reporting.

5

MEMORIES OF SPIRITUAL CONNECTIONS TO OUR SOURCE

∽ My friend Buckminster Fuller once remarked, "Everyone is born a genius, but the process of living de-geniuses them." Every child comes into this world in a state of perfection. They are new arrivals in form only; their true essence is as a piece of the infinite consciousness that we call by many names, the most common being "God." Before they have been exposed to all of the lessons that focus on their limitations, they are a grand source of wisdom and inspiration.

I have spent many an hour in my lifetime gazing into the wise eyes of newborns and asking them to teach me what I have forgotten because I allowed myself to become "de-geniused" along the way. I take every utterance that flows unedited from the mouths of babes and assume it has something to teach me.

In this chapter, you will read many accounts of small children who speak of their own personal memories of having a connection to their Source of being before they ever arrived here on Earth. The reason little boys and girls are often found to express what we adults call "unparalleled ingenuity" when it comes to matters of the soul, is only because they have not yet been hypnotized by the notion of limitations of any sort. They state precisely what they know to be true for them: They are unconcerned with what anyone else has come to believe, or if what they are saying might not be in agreement with what has come to be common knowledge. They speak from a place of certainty about something that they genuinely feel, and then, most frequently, simply go on with life as a young innocent being. It's as if, for a brief moment, they don't experience the earthly reality that surrounds them, but rather have this wondrous awareness of their infinite nature, which they feel completely free to express spontaneously.

Many of the children cited here refer to the idea of light as a representation of the formless world that they are recalling. When we first decided to put this compendium together, it was instigated by the remark of Dee's son, Marcus, who at 18 months of age simply raised his arms upward and said the word "Light," when asked about what God was like. In the very intense past-life regression session that I wrote about in *Wishes Fulfilled,* I recall seeing a beautiful, pleasurable light so dazzling and shimmering that I felt it behind my tightly closed eyes. This was an all-encompassing illumination that I have never forgotten, nor have I ever had it replicated since. As I felt myself attempting to describe in words what the experience of being in contact with my Source beyond this material plane was like, all I could see and feel was this resplendent light that was pure rapture.

What you will read here in this chapter is only a small sprinkling of the massive number of responses we received from parents and grandparents from all over the globe. It seems to be a universal truth that very young children frequently speak of a connection to another realm, where love, light, and compassion are the dominant themes of their inner remembering.

At two years old, my daughter was a very unusual child. For example, she had an extraordinary vocabulary for her age. One day, while we were sitting at the kitchen table, I was playing some Tibetan Buddhist chanting. My daughter was listening very intently, standing up on her chair, and obviously paying close attention. I asked, "Tatiana, do you like that singing?" She said, "They aren't singing, Mama; they are making light." I will never forget this.

Tatiana hasn't stopped being an unusual and socially awkward child, and she is off the charts in intelligence. She struggles, however, with severe bipolar disorder. I often wonder if her auditory "hallucinations" may in fact just mean that she is very finely tuned in to realms that most of us can't perceive.

— **KATHRYN ALEXANDER**
Santa Fe, New Mexico

My two young children and I were visiting my aunt, who's not biological, but very close to the family and helped raise me. Her mother (whom I used to call "Grandma") died when I was ten, and I always said I wanted to name my daughter after her. Well, while we were visiting, my daughter, who was three or four, told me, "Mommy, when I have a baby girl I want to name her Mariana." I'd never spoken to my daughter about Grandma's name, so we were all in shock.

Now my daughter is six, and in her we see an old soul, the peacekeeper, and my angel.

— **JENNIFER CULPEPPER-PALMER**
Fallon, New York

When my granddaughter was seven, I poured her a bowl of Rice Krispies. I was thinking about the "snap, crackle, pop" we all grew up with and said, "Listen when we pour the milk. What do you hear?"

She put her little head down to the bowl and said, "They're saying to meet Christopher." (Christopher was her precious 18-year-old uncle who was killed in an auto accident when she was 5. They were kindred spirits.) "They are saying to meet Christopher at the life bridge."

I was stunned. *Life bridge* is not a term I had ever used with her. "When? When are you supposed to meet Christopher at the life bridge?"

She replied, "When I am 30."

She is now 14, and has been telling us about Spirit since she was 18 months old.

— **LINDA LEIGHTON**
Auburn, California

I was driving when from out of the blue my five-year-old son, Krish, said, "Mom, you know I have lived more lives than you, but isn't it funny that this time you are my mom?" When he was three, he talked about God and angels all the time and saw them everywhere. He also told me once that fruit tastes much juicier on the trees in God's home.

I lost my sister suddenly three years ago, and he doesn't remember anything about her. I recently told him that I had a sister but she is now an angel and with God. He immediately closed his eyes and said that it's kind of strange because she looked like a human in a purple sky whereas other angels look very different and they swoosh through the room.

Once a plate slipped from my hands, and as I was trying to catch it, it flew and almost hit my face and fell down. My son was watching and said, "God controlled that plate with His mind and saved you since you are a good person."

— **MONIKA GOYAL**
Mountain View, California

My children, who are five and seven, have many conversations about when they were "in Mama's belly." Most recently, my son asked my daughter, "Did you watch TV while you were in Mama's belly?" When my daughter said no, Noah replied, "Well, I did."

Then I asked him, "Did you see me while you were in my belly?" Noah said, "No, but I imagined what you would look like." I asked, "Is this what you imagined I would look like?" He said, "No, you're prettier than I imagined."

— **STEPHANIE WAUTIER**
Marquette, Michigan

My father passed away in 2007 after a five-year battle with cancer. He and I had always been very close, even after my parents' divorce, when I moved with my mother to a different state at the age of seven. He liked to say that he knew we were soul mates the day I was born.

About a month after Dad died, I took my two-and-a-half-year-old daughter, Alexis, to the beach. Usually she enjoyed making "pizza" in the sand, but on this day, she announced, "Mama, I want to make something for Papa!"

"Okay, what do you want to make him?"

"An owl . . . no, I want to make him a bridge!"

A bridge, I thought, *that's odd. I've never heard her talk about a bridge before.* I said, "Okay, why a bridge?"

"Because it's okay, because everything's okay!"

I got chills at this point and asked, "Where does this bridge go?"

Without hesitation, and with much enthusiasm, she said, "It goes out to the water and up to the sky!"

— **AMY ALLERHEILIGEN WEISS**
Novato, California

I have three children: a daughter who is 13, a son with special needs and communication challenges who is 11, and another son who is 7.

My 11-year-old, James, seems to have quite a profound connection to Spirit. He is the gentlest, most compassionate soul I know. He tells me that he chats with God most nights when he's asleep, and a few years back he told my husband and me out of the blue that, with God, he chose us as his parents. He has described how he had a meeting with God before coming to Earth and how his soul traveled in some kind of vehicle. He also says that he remembers being in my tummy, and even "saw" the playroom that we were converting before he was born. He couldn't really have seen this once he was born, as we moved soon after I gave birth and we'd never mentioned it!

The most profound experience I have had with James came one night when I was especially worried about a situation and was praying so hard for help. My two boys were fast asleep on a sofa bed in our bedroom, and I stated to myself, "Jesus, please hear my prayer." James, who was fast asleep and couldn't have heard me because I was praying silently, whispered gently, "I am listening."

— **LOUISE McGRATH**
Manchester, United Kingdom

When I was pregnant with my son Cameron, I would always speak to him. (I did this with all my babies, as I felt a deep spiritual connection to them, and still do.) Two weeks before he was due, I lay there in bed with my hands stroking my tummy, and I said, "I know the doctors say you aren't due for a couple of weeks, but I'm ready for you to be born now if you are. So come now if you're ready." In that instant, my water broke with a loud sound, like a cork popping on a champagne bottle! Cameron was born a few hours later.

My midwife (and best friend) gave my son his first bath, and her eyes made contact with his. I remember her standing in the doorway, holding him wrapped in his little blanket, and asking him, "Who were you? You were here before, weren't you?" She said it was unusual for a newborn to engage in eye contact as he did. She said he was so knowing for a newborn baby. My Cameron is an old soul and has always lived in the moment.

— **MARY BINGHAM**
Holt, Australia

Meredith is our only child, and was extremely verbal very early on. One rushed and chaotic morning when she was three years old, we were on our way to my work and her preschool program, when we were involved in a horrible car accident. The minivan that I was driving had flipped on the interstate, and we were trapped in the car. Good Samaritans seemed to drop out of the sky to provide us with assistance; blessedly, Meredith was completely safe and uninjured, and I only ended up with a small cut that required a few stitches. There were no other people impacted. The first thing that the police officer said to me was, "I can't believe there wasn't a fatality in this accident. You are very lucky."

A month later, while decorating our home for the upcoming Christmas holiday, I pulled out our nativity scene, and Meredith helped me display it. As we went through the figures, I was explaining to her who was who (at this point, my husband and I had not introduced her to the Catholic Church we belonged to). When we got to the baby Jesus, she asked, "That's baby Jesus?" I said yes, and she said, "Oh, you know, he protected us in the accident."

I was a little taken aback by this, but I said that I thought she was right about that. Then I asked her how she knew that (again, she had no exposure to church or religion at that point in her young life). She said, "His Father told me." I asked her when she met his Father. Very matter-of-factly, she said, "Oh, I didn't meet Him. He talks to me in my head, when I'm going to sleep at night. His Father told me I never have to be scared, that Jesus would always protect us."

I was shocked, but felt sure that my daughter must have heard something at preschool, or maybe her teacher had discussed something with the class. When I inquired, though, her teacher quickly informed me that there were no discussions at school like this—due to the religious diversity of the class, they avoided such topics altogether.

It took quite a while for this conversation to really seep in for my husband and me, but we are convinced that Meredith had (and now, at age 29, continues to have) a very real connection with Spirit.

— **LAURA SCIARRIO**
Londonderry, New Hampshire

When my granddaughter, Erica, was four, we were sitting in front of my old farmhouse just enjoying the day. She suddenly jumped up from her chair, walked a few steps, and then turned to face me. Clasping her wee hands in front of her, she said, "I have something to tell you." She looked upward over her left shoulder in silence, then turning to me, said, "We all have the same mother. Your mother had a mother, and her mother had a mother, and on and on 'til we only have one mother."

I wanted to ask her to wait while I ran for a paper and pen but knew that would spoil something very sacred, so I just listened. At the end of each thought, Erica would pause, look upward over her left shoulder for about ten seconds, then turn once again to me. She said that if she came to the door of a stranger and knocked, they would not let her enter, but what they didn't realize is that we're all the same and there are no strangers. Another upward glance then, "God made the world and everything in the world." She closed with this quote: "He knows what is coming next."

She sat down beside me again, and I knew she was a gift to our family.

— **KAREN McINTOSH**
Ontario, Canada

When I was several months pregnant with my son, Elliot, I traveled to Kauai with some dear friends. We visited a sacred beach that is considered to be a portal where souls both enter and depart the earth. When my son was under the age of two, we were having a casual lunch conversation and I asked him if he remembered where he was before he came here to be a person. He looked up into space for a moment, then to me, and nonchalantly said, "Yes, Momma, Hawaii."

— **AHLEA KHADRO**
San Diego, California

My friend shared a story with me about her daughter, "Miss Three." As they were traveling in the car, Miss Three asked, "Is this real or is this imagination?" My friend asked her for clarification, and she replied, "The world, is it real or is it imagination?" My friend replied that she believed it was real.

Miss Three then asked, "Why do we have all this stuff?" She wanted to know why we had all of these material things (and pointed to several items as they drove by) and why we needed them. My friend tried to answer her questions, then she asked if everyone dies. "Yes," replied her mother. Miss Three said that "they go to see God and then come back." My friend has been brought up in a Christian faith and does not believe in reincarnation.

This little gorgeous girl has done other things that make me think she has a strong connection to the Other Side. When she was a baby, I once witnessed her standing on her cot, chatting to an invisible person. Her conversation was baby babbling, but she seemed delighted with the other . . . whatever or whomever she was having the conversation with.

Another time she asked her mother, "Who's that?" pointing at nothing. My friend replied there was nobody there. Miss Three asked again, and her mother repeated that nobody was there. This did not stop her from going up the driveway to chat with whoever she thought she was seeing.

— **TANIA FREW**
Queensland, Australia

My son's twin sister passed away two months after they were born. When he was two, he asked me if he would go back to the light like his sister. I cried and told him that we all return to the light. Now he says that he will know his sister again someday.

— **JAHDESS CLARKE-MAHONEY***

My son, Tony, age three, and I were riding down the highway, and he was looking out the window. This was before children had to be in the backseat. He was whispering, apparently to the clouds.

I asked, "What are you saying? I can't hear you."

"I'm not talking to you."

"Who are you talking to?"

"Jesus."

Now, I want to clarify that I had not taught my son about Jesus. I personally prayed, but I had not "brainwashed" him. So this came out of left field, completely.

I cautiously asked, "Was he talking back?"

"Yes."

"What was he saying?"

"He was saying he made the clouds."

"Why do you look so unhappy?"

"Because I used to be with him. Now he just talks to me."

A month later we were floating on inner tubes, enjoying a lazy river in Utah, and when we got to this one beautiful spot, my son perked up, all excited. He said, "Jesus's father painted these mountains!"

By now I'd been hearing him tell stories of talking to Jesus regularly, yet I was still surprised to hear this new tidbit. I asked, "Jesus's father? You mean God?" Tony frowned, shook his head, and said, "No, his other father. He painted these mountains. I watched him do it before I came here to be with you." I can only guess he must have meant Joseph.

It was not the only shock of the day. We floated the river two more times, and although he was almost asleep in my lap in the inner tube, each time we passed through that particular section of the river, my son perked up and repeated, word for word, the same message.

Intrigued by his Jesus talk, I took Tony into a Christian bookstore and found a wall of postcards with various depictions of Christ and other biblical figures. I thought I'd let him have a picture of Jesus if he wanted one. He did want one, but he fished through the whole assortment, rejecting most. He knows what Jesus looked like and wasn't satisfied until he found the exact picture he wanted. My son is 24 now and still cherishes that picture.

— **JENNIFER DICAMILLO**
Highlandsville, Missouri

My two-year-old son is constantly talking about the people in white. Once I asked him to tell me about them, and he said they come at night a lot and watch over him. He said they are like "light," and when they leave he gets very sad.

— **ANN INIGUEZ**
Lynchburg, Virgina

When my son, Pietro, was two years old, he asked me questions about his cousin who was still in her mommy's belly. I told Pietro that he was in *my* belly and asked him if he could remember. He said that he could.

"What do you remember?" I asked. "What was inside with you?"

"Water."

"What could you see?"

"Light."

"What did you hear?"

"Mommy and Daddy," he responded.

He was just starting to speak, so his answers were very simple, yet decisive.

— **SIMONA BOLLO**
Azeglio, Italy

A few days before I found out I was pregnant, my mom dreamed of my grandmother (who had passed away a few days earlier). She was holding a baby boy's hand, and he had beautiful blue eyes. She told my mom to "tell Mehrzad to take care of him—he is an amazing gift."

When my son, Nima, was three years old, two shocking events happened. First, my dear aunt passed away. When my son found out, he closed his eyes and said, "Auntie is with Grandma in a beautiful triangle of blue light." I asked him, "What is the triangle light?" He said that it was God.

A few weeks later we went to Iran, where my grandmother used to live with my other aunt. Nima insisted on visiting Grandma's room. As soon as he went in, he started touching a few of her belongings (praying cloth, rosary, and photos). He was smiling and laughing, talking out loud to her and asking her about the light. It was as if he was seeing it with her. We were all speechless. I know he remembered the light he came from.

— **MEHRZAD ZAMANPOUR***

When my daughter was six weeks old, I was rocking her and looked right down into her eyes, and this most beautiful light came out of her, which I had never seen before. This was the brightest light I had ever seen, yet it didn't even hurt my eyes. This light went into me—the illumination went into me and made me feel so peaceful.

Here is my take on this: My daughter came into my life to give me some of heaven's light (she had just come from there), and this light was going to be enough to sustain me until I left this earth again.

— **MARY BARTLETT**
Canton, Massachusetts

Recently, my two-and-a-half-year-old daughter was very sick for three days with an unknown stomach virus. We were visiting doctors, and she had to have a painful catheter that was rather traumatic. In trying to comfort her, I told her that when I was little I was really sick one time, too—I was in the hospital, getting poked and prodded, and was feeling terrible.

She looked at me and said, "I was there with you."

"What do you mean that you were there with me?"

"I was there holding you, and helping you feel all better."

Since then, she has mentioned holding my hand when I was a little girl at certain times (mostly at times when I had fallen down). I've always called her my angel baby, but never thought it could be meant so literally.

— **JESSICA REEVES POTASZ**
Colorado Springs, Colorado

I am the mother of two daughters. Ever since my eldest, Adi, was very little (she's now six), I've felt that she has a special gift and remembers her time in Spirit like it was a memory from yesterday. I think she believes that everyone functions on that plane—that is, one foot on the physical plane and one foot always connected to the Divine and the world of Spirit. I actually believe she is an Earth angel.

There are times I look at her after she says these things, expecting her to say, "Ha, the joke's on you, Mom!" because I am just blown away, but she never does. I work hard as her mom to help her honor her gift. I am constantly amazed and inspired.

Adi has always said some very funny and interesting things. I started writing them down when she was very young, and have compiled a few snippets of the things that have so casually and pragmatically come out of her mouth:

> • She has said, "Mom, when there are sunrises and sunsets, that is heaven smiling at us."

> • The other night, she told me "Mom, did you know there is a baby born every second?" When I replied, "Well, I guess I didn't know that. Who told you that?" she said, "God told me." I asked if she heard His voice, and she said, "No, it's a feeling in my heart."

> • After praying before our dinner, Adi asked, "Dad, why are you *so* loud when praying?" I jokingly said, "To make sure God can hear you," and she responded, "You don't have to be loud; God always

hears you." Her dad asked, "Are you an angel on Earth?" and she said, "Yes, I am."

• One night while our family was talking about her great-granddad who had just passed away, Adi said, out of the blue, "God wanted him home."

— **KARYN WILLIAMS**
Westrichland, Washington

My daughter is five years old, and I had her after five miscarriages. I used to write in a journal to her years before I was pregnant. The first entry was July 14, 2008; she was born two years to that day after that. As we were going to bed recently, she told me that she sees colored sparks of light that come from heaven and go through her skin. I told her it may be angels, and she fell asleep. Not an hour later I tuned in to Dr. Dyer's radio show and heard about this book. Children are truly Divine.

— **HEATHER McLELLAN**
San Carlos, California

I was close to my Source until almost the age of six. I once lost a polished rock in an alfalfa field when playing, and I cried like my heart was broken. My mother told me to think really hard about the rock and walk to where I'd dropped it. I did just that and managed to find that small rock in the huge alfalfa field. My family was speechless when I came home with it. I trusted what my mother said with the open heart of a child connected to my Source.

When I was seven, we moved to town and I started second grade. My father did shift work and was home at 5 P.M. for supper—you were expected to be in your seat with your hands washed and ready when he walked in the door. I was on my way home after school and jumped up on a retaining wall because I liked to balance on top. I must have fallen off and passed out, and when I came to, it was getting dark.

When I got home, my mother told me my father had left again for work and was not happy. Standing there with my bloody hair, I launched into this story: "Momma, I fell and went to this place and there were all of these people there! Well, they were people, but they didn't have edges! They knew me, Momma, and I knew them, too, but you don't. I knew everything, Momma, and there weren't even any questions! They loved me so much and I wanted to just stay there and float, but they told me I had to go. Then just like that I was back!"

I've read other people's stories about their near-death experiences, and some speak to me and others don't. It was dark where I went and not full of bright lights or angels—no tunnels or people as I see them here.

During one of his State of the Union addresses, I heard President Obama say this quote from the Bible: "I knew and I was known." I stopped in my tracks. That is what it was like for me when I transcended. All those beautiful souls knew me, and loved me with such a love as I've never known here on Earth. It was delicious. It was like a reunion where you meet people you forgot you knew . . . eons of loving souls that you join again.

— **JANIS COX AHERN**
Plymouth, New Hampshire

❧ Young children are filled with Divine spiritual wisdom. I encourage you to spend as much quality time with these new arrivals as possible. Get down on the floor and be with them at their level, as I have done so often myself. Look them directly in the eye and speak to them not as an equal, but as a student inquiring of a spiritual master. A child who feels safe and adored is much more likely to speak of their own unique inner knowings about the world beyond this physical domain.

Throughout my life I have always opted for the company of children over small talk from adults. Tiny newborns are intriguing to me, and playing with little toddlers has always brought me so much joy. The great Russian novelist Fyodor Dostoyevsky once said, "The soul is healed by being with children." I believe this is so because children have not yet adopted a set of beliefs about who they are and what is impossible. They live from their soul and, by doing so, remind us adults about who we truly are as well—that is, spiritual beings having temporary human experiences, rather than the reverse.

CHAPTER

6

MYSTICAL AND PRECOGNITIVE WISDOM

∽ When my daughter Sommer was about two years of age, and just beginning to talk with her own unique pronunciation of words, she approached a woman in her early 20s who was visiting our home, pointed directly at her stomach, and said, "I see dat baby in dare." Years later we found out the young woman had just discovered that she was pregnant, and had made her own decision to terminate that unwanted pregnancy because she had been raped several months earlier. This book's sixth chapter relates a number of brief stories in which very young children demonstrate a kind of psychic wisdom that defies all rational explanation.

I myself have had quite a few of these inexplicable awarenesses at various times in my life. I recall as a young father being awakened from a deep sleep in the front seat of our automobile while my wife was driving, with two children also asleep in the backseat. I suddenly opened my eyes, looked up, and saw that a car was in the wrong lane of the two-lane highway and heading directly toward the car in front of us. As the car in front swerved to avoid a head-on collision, I grabbed the steering wheel, preventing an impact that very likely would have resulted in several deaths.

I have said many times to audiences all over the world, "If prayer is you talking to God, then intuition is God talking to you." I cannot answer the question of what it was that caused me to awaken from that deep sleep in the exact moment that I was needed to avoid a tragedy way back in 1971, nor can I explain why so many children seem to have such highly developed intuitive powers that allow them to say the things they do.

I do know that these stories about the mysticlike wisdom that flows from our children provide fascinating anecdotal evidence of intelligence from a spiritual dimension experienced prior to their arrival here on Earth. I have often said that when you learn to trust in yourself, you are actually trusting in the very wisdom that created you. From their earliest efforts at talking and cognizing, children have no one else to trust in but themselves. They feel something inside and blurt it out, and all those who hear these sagacious words are befuddled and mystified. They are truly trusting in the same infinite wisdom that brought them from the formless world of Spirit into this physical world of beginnings and endings.

One of my all-time favorite romantic poets of the early 19th century, Samuel Taylor Coleridge, once penned these words that I encourage you to consider as you read these sparkling accounts of the wisdom of our children: "The history of a man for the nine months preceding his birth would, probably, be far more interesting and contain events of greater moment than all the three score and ten years that follow it."

When my youngest brother was just three years old in 1967, we were all at the dinner table with him in his high chair. Out of nowhere he looked at my mother and said, "You have a sick tummy." She was shocked and asked, "How do you know that?" My brother answered, "God told me." She was diagnosed a few days later with an infected gallbladder and had to have emergency surgery.

— **CHRISTINA TURNER**
Hillsborough, New Jersey

When I first found out I was pregnant with my son, my daughter was four. She didn't know yet, and I was wondering how to tell her. She looked at me and said, "I'm going to have a little brother," and then went about her business.

— **NICOLE GRAHAM**
San Diego, California

My daughter was about eight when we were driving past a field where vultures were flying high in a circle. I made the comment that something must have died below them. My daughter asked me if I knew why they were flying so high in circles. I responded by asking what her thoughts were. She hesitated for just a few seconds and then told me that they fly in a circle waiting for the animal's soul to leave. It was such an unexpected yet powerful statement. Our children are here to further awaken us if we take the time to listen.

— **TRACY REECE**
San Antonio, Texas

Thirty years ago, my five-and-a-half-year-old son, Kevin, went home to the good Lord after having an intraventricular hemorrhage in his brain. Just months prior to his passing, my brother-in-law had asked him to be the ring bearer at his wedding, but Kevin said that he would not be there. And when I was buying him new school clothes for kindergarten, he told me that he would never go to school, or live anywhere other than where we were living at the time.

From Kevin's conception through today, my son changed my life—and he remains a constant reminder that the true meaning of life, and its purpose, is about love.

— **BETTY JEAN GUSHANAS**
Princeton, New Jersey

One day when my daughter was four, she told me to look at the sun. I said, "Yes, honey, it's so pretty!" She replied, "Do you see the ribbons, Mommy? The light ribbons go into everyone's hearts and fill them with love."

— **DALE-ANNE BERNSTEIN***

I am a single mom of three fantastic daughters. Two of my daughters are older and off on their own; my youngest, Cali, has just turned four.

Cali, in this dimension, does not have any grandparents. My mother passed away in 1985 when I was only 17, long before I was married or divorced. Yet my daughter has often gone on and on about this mysterious "Grandma" that she has. When she talks about it, if I say "Grandmother," she corrects me. "No, Mum, it's *Grandma!*"

I have an uncle who is very ill. On the way home from a trip to visit him, I asked my older daughter, Olivia, and her boyfriend, Dimitrious, if they minded if we stopped by the cemetery where my mother was buried. Cali had never been there before, and earlier in the week I had been trying to explain to her about heaven and what happens when animals die. She had been playing very roughly with Olivia's little dog, Chief, and I was afraid that she didn't know the consequences of this. I thought visiting the cemetery might make things a little easier to understand.

When we arrived, I was amazed by the vast number of gravestones that had been placed since the last time I had been there (about three years before). Where my mother had been, in what was once the third row back, was now fronted by hundreds of the newly deceased. Olivia and I stood dumbfounded, as we could not find the headstone. Cali took off running through the gravestones, in the complete opposite direction of her sister and me. Cali is a high-energy girl, and I figured this was going to be a game of cat and mouse to get her to come with us. I turned to give chase, when suddenly she stopped in her tracks. With her finger pointed and arm outstretched, she yelled, "Here it is!" In a place she had never been before, among rows and rows of identical headstones, with pinpoint accuracy, Cali had found my mother's gravesite.

I think we stood there in awe for a good five to ten minutes, trying to really absorb the situation. I still get goose bumps when I talk about it. Of course, Cali had no explanation of how she knew . . . she just shrugged her shoulders and continued to play nearby.

— **EILEEN LEDONNE**
Lynn, Massachusetts

When my son Michael Gabriel was a baby and I'd put him to sleep, I could hear him giggle and giggle through the baby talk like someone was tickling him or playing with him. When he was three years old, he knocked something down in the basement. As I came to the stairs, I said, "Michael, that's a bad boy!" He replied, "I am not a bad boy! I am a piece of love." I was amazed! It was so nicely and correctly said—and a few years ago when reading *Wishes Fulfilled* and *The "I AM" Discourses,* I could see clearly how right my three-year-old was. He is very kind, loving, and full of joy.

When I was pregnant with my third child, my son was six at the time (he's now ten) and asked me, "What if there are two babies?" I said, "No, there will be just one." The idea of having the blessing of twins had never crossed my mind.

He was right—the twins are now four years old and very sweet!

— **ROSE C. CICHOCKI**
Easton, Pennsylvania

My friend Summer was driving on a major interstate with her two children. Her 12-year-old daughter was in the front seat, and her 4-year-old son, Blake, was strapped in a car seat in the back.

They were driving along, listening to the radio, and then from out of the blue, Blake leaned forward and said, "Mommy, whatever happens, I love you."

She looked at him in the rearview mirror and said, "I love you, too, Blake. Are you okay?"

"Yes."

They drove for a few more miles in silence, and Summer wondered what had prompted that remark. Suddenly, the driver of a tractor-trailer lost control and jackknifed in front of them. Summer slammed on the brakes, but her small car ended up going underneath the truck, which dragged them for almost a hundred yards down the highway. The roof of her car was crushed in, pinning them inside. It took hours for the emergency-response team to cut them out of the car, yet aside from some minor cuts and bruises, they were all okay.

It seems that Blake had intuitively known that something was going to go wrong, and just wanted his mom to know he loved her.

— **MARGRETHE KROGH**
Knoxville, Tennessee

My daughter, Angelica, was born with the wisest eyes— the kind of eyes that are scanning through your soul, only to add compassion and love into your system.

When Angelica was a baby, she was always happy to go for rides in my car. Yet after one half-hour drive, she started screaming like a maniac. As we were in the fast lane going quite quickly, I pulled over to the shoulder and stopped, thinking that a bee might have stung her. When I gathered her in my arms, she stopped crying abruptly and stared at me.

I then heard a huge crash, the biggest I had ever experienced in Athens. A truck had lost control and smashed the cars in all the lanes with many deaths involved. It took several hours to move our car, but Angelica and I found a way to enjoy our day together. She remained calm the entire time.

— **SALOME**
East Sussex, United Kingdom

My son, Lucas, now age thirteen, declared something profound when he was two and a half. My parents, my husband, our new baby girl, Lucas, and I were sitting outdoors on a family vacation, playing with clay and having quite a moment. Lucas suddenly said, "Everything is love. It's all about love. We are all made of love and God is love." (We are not a family who talks much about God.)

Stunned, I replied, "Lucas, what a beautiful thing to say. Where did you hear that?" After a pause, he said, "I already knew it when I came here."

Four adults and one baby heard him say this, and we all cried! I have tears running down my face just remembering it. I hope you enjoy it, too.

— **ANASTASIA BRIEN**
Greenwich, Connecticut

My bright and multitalented daughter, Signe, is now middle-aged. When she was just a little toddler, she simply would not stay in her crib when I put her to bed at night, and repeatedly showed up in the living room to take part in activities there.

One night after tucking her in for the umpteenth time, I looked down at her with exasperation and said, "Signe, what am I going to do with you?"

"Just love me, Mommy," was her oh-so-wise reply.

Out of the mouth of a babe came Divine wisdom. To this day, she does not remember it, but I do.

— **BONNIE DEFRIEST**
Philomath, Oregon

My daughter spoke of a gray coat, a waterfall, and a brass bed when she was three. My husband paled and admitted that his mother had the coat and the bed, and she lived near a waterfall in Ireland before she passed. The comfort of this knowledge has brought all things into perspective.

— **SUSAN CLAUDIA MORRISON**
Spokane Valley, Washington

When my son was about four, he was outside with me while I was gardening on an overcast, drizzly day. I grumbled about the weather, and he tugged on my sleeve and said sternly, "Mummy, don't you know there is always a rainbow? You just can't see it because of the clouds." He totally floored me with this!

— **ROSALIE OLDING**
Victoria, Australia

I was having a tea party with my four-and-a-half-year-old granddaughter, Mia, last week. I had a photo of my mother (who passed away 15 years ago) on a nearby stand; Mia asked me to include her in the tea party, and I obliged. This began a short conversation about life. First she requested that I put the teacup up to Nana's mouth so she could have a drink. Then she stated in a matter-of-fact way that "Nana is in heaven with God."

I said, "Yes. Tell me more."

Mia said, "Then you come back here and start all over again." Like it is so simple . . . what a gem!

— **LIZ LORING**
Cincinnati, Ohio

My son was very quick to learn to talk, walk, and string words together to form sentences. At the age of three, he asked, "When we die, are we born again?" For a three-year-old to ask a question on death and birth totally amazed me! I still remember that spine-tingling feeling.

— **JOJO LOWEY**
Ayrshire, Scotland

When my daughter, Emily, was about 3 (she's now 22), I reprimanded her for something. To which she replied, "I'm not my brain, you know!" She was spot-on!

— **TANYA DANNOCK**
Nicholls, Australia

My four-year-old daughter, Lily, recently saw a photo on my cell phone of a close family friend who had just undergone emergency brain surgery following a bicycle accident. A car traveling over 25 mph had hit Frankie, who sadly wasn't wearing his helmet (it was on the handlebars). After the accident, all of the first responders and the medical staff said that there was really not any "reason" that Frankie should have survived this accident. His mother immediately requested prayers from everyone she could reach.

I had no intention for my four-year-old to see the fairly graphic photo on my phone (it was for my older daughters to learn from—wear your helmet!). Yet Lily did see the picture, and then almost went into a trance. She immediately started running her fingers right along the line of staples and stitches on the boy's head; she just kept rubbing on them and staring at him. She said, "Mom, we need to pray for him," and went into an impromptu prayer for Frankie. I was so moved that I asked if I could record the prayer and send it to him to hear. She agreed and recited another prayer into my phone.

I get chills when I listen back to my four-year-old ask God to heal Frankie and his head, and her assertion that he needed "calm, quiet, dark, and rest to heal, and to also eat healthy food!" The next day Frankie's mom posted an update on her son, saying that it was a miracle how fast he was healing. And then she said, "The doctor has said that Frankie will need a calm, quiet, and dimly lit environment and plenty of rest to heal."

Wow. This is almost word for word what Lily, I feel, channeled as Frankie's prescription for healing. He went home six days later with no long-term damage at all.

— **KRISTI INZUNZA**
San Diego, California

When my son, Daniel, was about two years old, he told me that when we are born, we know everything, but as we grow up, we forget. It blew me away so much that I still remember it.

— **LESLEY TIMMS**
West Midlands, United Kingdom

Here are a few stories that my daughter, Jaiyda, shared with me in her first three and a half years of life:

• "Mommy, did you know that the universe is in your heart? All you have to do is look in and look at it and feel it. It is right in front of you, not behind you."

• "Mommy, your grandpa Al likes to watch over me at bedtime with the angels. He likes purple flowers, just like me. He likes to show you purple flowers." My grandpa passed away over 20 years ago and she never even knew his name. It blew me away.

• "Mommy, God is energy. Angels are energy. They are bright lights in my heart and everyone's heart."

• "I was free and used to fly. Why can't I fly here on Earth? It was like clouds up in the sky, everything and anything, everywhere and anywhere."

• "Mommy, I sometimes have not my voice in my head. It doesn't sound like me . . . I know it is a whisper from someone telling me to do something good. I think it might be God's voice."

— **JANELLE STREETER***

My daughter is eight. The other day she told me, "Mama, in the next era when we have new life, we will still look like humans—but we will have new minds, and we will be kind to each other, and we will love nature, and we will live with the trees in tree houses and we will be happy." I find this extraordinary because we've never discussed ideas like this.

She also frequently references our past life together and our next lives. If she is particularly happy, she looks and reaches for the sky. I marvel at her and at the beauty of her conscious connection to God.

— KRISTINE ACKERMAN SPERLING
Santa Barbara, California

When my son, Jade, was six years old, a friend was staying with us and started to write a journal on the words of wisdom that came from his young mouth. Here are a few of the quotes that were recorded:

• *Jade believes in past lives, but says it is too complicated to explain, as all lives happen at the same time.*

• *He says, "When the cup's upside-down, part of your God is caught in it. God helps the universe, makes us think, puts thinking in our minds, makes the wind blow, and so on, and God is doing everything at the same time. God is everywhere—He is even in bad people—and helps us grow."*

• *Jade says that he sees circles a lot, gray in color, with white bits in them. Sometimes they are joined by a line, sometimes not. He says they are probably atoms that are splitting, and the reason they do that is to give the earth energy. He says that these gray circles aren't angels because angels have sparkles and so do nature spirits. He said that it isn't energy because energy moves very fast in a straight line.*

I think that is enough to give you an idea of Jade's fascinating mind and soul in 1989, at the age of six. Interestingly enough, when he turned seven, this all stopped.

— **DIANE KALLEND**
Hobart, Tasmania, Australia

My wife was about ten weeks pregnant with our second boy, and we had not shared the news with anybody yet. One day our firstborn, who was about two and a half years old at the time, touched my wife's belly and said, "Momma, baby in stomach."

— **RALPH RENZ**
Brooklyn, New York

While sitting by a lake watching the ducks take off and land, my seven-year-old said, "When I die I want to go and check out the duck spirits because they look fun."

I didn't answer, and then he asked me, "When you die, will you come and visit me?"

I was intrigued by his questions and replied, "Honey, I'll be dead way before you. You have a long and happy life ahead of you."

Not happy with my reply, he insisted, "But will you come and find me when you die?"

Two weeks later he developed nephritic syndrome—without prednisone and several weeks in the hospital, we would have lost him. Somehow he already knew.

— **RUTH CARTER**
Kapiti Coast, New Zealand

In 1994 I participated in a "Life, Death, and Transition" workshop facilitated by Elisabeth Kübler-Ross. I was grieving some of my own losses and found that this was really the opportunity to come to terms with my perspective of life and death, and my purpose in it. This cantankerous Swiss powerhouse shared her belief that we have a precognition of when and even how we will pass, telling us that it is sometimes evident in artwork done before a person's passing.

Dr. Kübler-Ross told us the story of a pregnant mom expecting her third child. She had taken her five- and seven-year-old daughters on a weekend adventure to a seaside cottage they had never visited before, which was a few hours from their home. Here they planned to share some special time together before the new baby was to be born, and the father was planning to join them after he got off work.

After the long solo drive, the mom carried things into the cottage while the girls played in the quaint yard surrounded by a picket fence. She was tired from the long drive and keeping little ones entertained, so she sat down for a few minutes and unintentionally dozed off. She was awakened from her nap by hysterical screaming, and followed the chaotic voices to the water's edge. All too soon it became clear that one of her children had not only waded out into the water, but had been attacked by a shark. The seven-year-old girl died.

Fortunately, this distraught woman eventually found her way to Elisabeth for help in making sense of the tragedy. Elisabeth asked her to bring to their meeting any artwork her daughter might have done just prior to her passing. The mom brought three drawings that her eldest daughter had done in the car on the drive to the seashore. The first was of the two little girls playing in the fenced yard of the cottage. Neither of the girls had ever seen the cottage, nor was what it would look like shared with them; however, this picture had all the detailed features, including the picket fence. The second drawing was of the two little girls playing alone by the water's edge. In the third drawing the smallest child stood alone on the shore. Her sister was nowhere to be seen . . . but even more chilling was the fact that there was a shark's fin in the water offshore.

— **RHONDA HULL, PH.D.**
Port Townsend, Washington

My son, Maximus, is definitely an old soul. He is five now and always keeps me on my toes, yet he is very careful and makes sure that his little twin sisters are safe. One time when he was three, I was telling him that his sisters were both in my belly at the same time. He nonchalantly explained that if I had had three babies in my belly, I would have died.

Maximus was a triplet, but the other two didn't make it (early on in my pregnancy). He actually gave me the answer I so desperately needed to hear and understand. I feel that my twin girls are the original souls I lost and came back to me when it was the right time.

— **CARMEN PERDOMO ESCUDERO**
Coral Gables, Florida

When my son, Chris, was around five years old, I dropped him off at a friend's birthday party. When I picked him up afterward, he told me that his friend's older brother had told him that there was no Santa Claus, and asked me if that was true. I did not want to lie to my son, but at the same time I didn't want to take that childhood fantasy away from him so soon. So I said, "Well, just because you can't see him doesn't mean that he's not real." Chris replied, "Just like God?" and I said, "Yes, just like God."

Then he said the strangest thing: "I think we all have a piece of God in us." I asked him who told him that, and he said nobody. I asked him again because I couldn't believe that was coming from a five-year-old who had no religious training whatsoever. He told me again that nobody had told him, and I could tell by the look on his face that he was telling the truth.

That happened 23 years ago, but I will never forget it because there was something so magical about that moment.

— **BARBARA ROLL-GIELEGHEM**
Hillsborough, New Jersey

My seven-year-old son said to me last week, "Mum, do you ever feel like you're not real?"

I replied, "Do you mean that you feel like you're in a dream but you're awake?"

His face lit up at being understood. "Yes, like this whole world is a dream." He then talked about how the "real" part of him is that love inside that is always with God.

He has an understanding at seven of who he really is that I am only now discovering in my thirties.

— **JEN HABJAN**
North Warrandyte, Australia

In December 1985 my son Alan was born. He managed to get hung up in the birth canal and breathed in fluids; the doctors had to keep him elevated in an upside-down position for two hours before we could hold him. His big brother, Andrew, was two years old and was really excited to get "my friend here to play with me again."

Alan was a very healthy little man after all the work it took to get him here. He progressed rather quickly, walking by seven months and speaking with a good vocabulary by one year. I liked to take my children to rest homes to visit the elderly, like my parents did with me. Between the ages of two and five, Alan would talk in detail to these gentlemen about war battles, boats, and life. Once he even sat there calmly with an old veteran, going into full detail on how to break down an M1917 Enfield rifle! The older gentleman and I were fascinated by how a three-year-old could know this.

Sometimes things got downright eerie. It was during this time that Alan started saying he was a "short timer" and mentioned his need "to go home" quite a bit. He also said that "death does not hurt, and we have all died many times already." When my father died, he told me, "Papa John is just fine now and not the old guy stuck in his bed anymore."

In October 2008, Alan took his life. He was a healthy and happy young man, not depressed—life was good—and it was a shock to everyone. I was a mess when it happened, but then I heard Alan say, "Mom, quit your blubbering." And I realized it was not about me; he had "to go home." His death was about his need to continue to grow. He came into this world for a short time to help those he loved—and continues to love.

— **MARY LAUD**
Kalispell, Montana

≋ As adults, it is a common misconception to view children as if they were "apprentice people" on their way to becoming fully human when they ultimately arrive at adulthood. I urge you to begin to look at all children as spiritual beings, offspring of an infinite system with all of the wisdom, powers, and capacities of the Source from which they originated. Every person is whole and complete in the now, regardless of the chronological age of the body. Consequently, no one has any more claim to being wiser simply because they are bigger and older.

With this kind of reprogramming, you can treat each young person you encounter with all of the respect due an evolved spiritual master. Rather than assuming that a child is too immature to have anything of real merit to offer, listen carefully instead, and then engage them if they are willing to expand upon anything that they have offered.

Every time I gaze at a newborn, I converse silently with them in awe of the wisdom that is their very essence. I suggest that as you look at a young child, you see the unfolding of an infinite consciousness before you. Trust that they have something of great value to offer you, particularly since they have not yet learned to doubt themselves.

I have always considered each of my children as my teacher on the subject of their own innate knowings, particularly when they speak of mystical or spiritual matters. Who am I to question what they feel deep within

7

INVISIBLE FRIENDS
AND SPIRITUAL
VISITATIONS

∽ The message of this chapter relates very specifically to experiences that I recall with two of my own children when they were very young.

My daughter Serena had an invisible (at least, to my wife and me) friend named Jesse who was her constant companion as a three-year-old. When my wife would set the table, Serena would always say, "Don't forget to set a place for Jesse." When she was taking a bath, she would devote a lot of attention to brushing Jesse's hair; in the car, she would tell her older siblings to move over and leave some room for Jesse. At night when she would say her prayers, she would always instruct either her mom or me to listen to not only her own prayers, but those of Jesse as well.

This was far more than just a childhood fantasy for our little girl—she could actually see Jesse, describing all of her features and what she was wearing, and would become very emotional if we didn't pay the proper attention to her friend. She would look at us in frustrated disbelief because we were unable to see with our eyes what was so obvious to Serena.

When my son Sands was a little boy, he experienced a visitation from an apparition that was shocking to him to say the least. I had written a book titled *A Promise Is a Promise,* about a young woman named Edwarda O'Bara who lived in a comatose state for more than 40 years. As Edwarda had slipped into the coma, her mother, Kaye, had promised her that she would never leave her. Her final words to her daughter were, "And a promise is a promise."

My wife and I had visited the O'Bara home on many occasions, and all of our children had been given an opportunity to come and be in their sacred home in Miami and pray with Edwarda. At that time, Kaye had spent a quarter of a century caring for her daughter in her home, and she told us that she knew when Edwarda would leave her body and do healing work all over the globe.

I'll never forget the night that Sands came running out of the bathroom, proclaiming that Edwarda was there with him in the shower. He had never heard any of the conversations we had had about Edwarda's out-of-body visitations, and yet he was absolutely adamant that he had seen her standing there smiling as he took a shower.

This chapter is replete with stories about children who have reported similar visitations. There might have been a time when such sightings would have been met with skepticism by me, but not any longer. Particularly since I had a middle-of-the-night visitation from my own deceased mother before I was to speak in Glasgow, Scotland, a couple of years back. I could see her sitting on the bed and smiling at me. I was astonished, since she had passed away just six weeks earlier, and said, "You can't be here, Mother—you're dead."

As those words came out, my mother went from being a vibrant, happy, 40-year-old woman to someone who aged instantly before my eyes, and then slowly vanished from the room. As I said the words "you're dead," she shook her head as if to say that there is no such thing as death, and she was gone. This was not an apparition or a dream; my mother was there in the room for those moments, and I was fully awake. I walked around the hotel room there in Scotland for several hours in amazed exultation at what had just transpired.

Dr. Marjorie Taylor, the author of *Imaginary Companions and the Children Who Create Them,* asserts that 65 percent of children under the age of seven have imaginary friends. If a child sees something that others cannot see, does that necessarily mean it does not exist? In all of the stories detailed here in this chapter, I have chosen to have an open mind. I've lived too many years now to entertain any doubts about this fascinating topic of spiritual visitations.

Before you dismiss any of these vignettes about children and their "imaginary" visitations as simply the results of overactive childhood fantasies and label them as impossible, take a hard look at that word *impossible*. When you break the word down it says, "I'm possible." And the contraction "I'm" of course means I AM, which is the name given to Moses when he asked for the name of the apparition speaking to him. I encourage you to read with an open mind and keep in mind that indeed, "I'm possible."

My youngest daughter, Holly, visited and played with her sister, Leah, for years—even though Leah had died six weeks after Holly was born. How did she know her? Holly talked about her sister in the present, and it would bother me so much that I would tell her to stop talking about Leah. Holly is a young woman now, and we talk about the fact that she did not know that Leah was dead when she was young.

— **ROXANNE PROTHERO BASFORD***

My youngest daughter was barely three years old in 1989 when our family moved into our temporary rental home in central Illinois. She immediately began talking about "that man" she would see in our house. She said that he was nice and played with her, and talked to her all the time. She would point and say, "See, Mom, see that man." The poor little thing would get so frustrated that we all couldn't see what she was looking at. She was a healthy, normal child in every way, but she definitely saw a man in that house.

After my husband and I gave notice that we were moving into a new home, the landlord was talking to us and revealed that the previous tenant, an elderly gentleman, had dropped dead suddenly of a heart attack in the kitchen. So we finally realized that our daughter had obviously been seeing the spirit of this deceased former tenant. Once we moved into our new home, she quit talking about it, and we all knew that something spiritual and beyond our realm had taken place that year in our old house.

Our daughter is now a grown woman and works as a pediatric RN, and she has lost all recollection of this experience.

— **PEGGY EPLEY***

My mother, Lois, passed away nine years before my son, Quinn, was born. My father remarried the next year. Once Quinn was able to talk, he would call my husband's mother "Nana" and my dad's wife "Grandma Hot Soup" (because she always fixed him soup). Meanwhile, I'd tell him stories of my mother, an amazing, fun person who was also my best friend.

One day I picked Quinn up from day care and was told that he actually took a nap, which he rarely did. On the way home, I asked this very expressive two-a-half-year-old about how he was able to fall asleep—what follows is how the conversation went.

Me: So that was good that you could take a nap. How did you settle down enough to do that?

Quinn: Grandma came and was patting my back.

Me (befuddled because you need an access card to get into the center): You mean Nana came to see you?

Quinn: No, the other grandma.

Me: Grandma Hot Soup came to see you?

Quinn: No, the other one. *Your* mom.

Me (hardly able to breathe): You mean Grandma Lois was there?

Quinn (very matter-of-factly): Yeah. She comes there a lot to see me because she knows I don't like to take naps.

Me: She does?

Quinn: Yeah. She's so nice. She patted my back for me until I fell asleep.

To this day, Quinn says he can see guardian angels around people, sitting on each shoulder. He says everyone has two. Of course, he is an amazing kid and a blessing.

— **CYNDY NEHR**
Grosse Pointe Woods, Michigan

This is a story my mother-in-law likes to tell: When my husband was quite young, he would often see the face of a man smiling. This happened when he closed his eyes or when he was on his own. Whenever his mum smiled, he would say, "You look like that man I see."

A few years later, my husband saw a photo of his granddad (his mum's dad), who had died when my mother-in-law was very young, and said, "That's the man who I saw all the time. He looks like you when you smile."

— **KATIONA MATTO**
Gibraltar, United Kingdom

My youngest son, Aaron, would always tell me that he'd go over the bridge to the Other Side, where he went fishing with a man and woman. When it was time for him to come back over the bridge, they would give him candy bars for the ride back.

One day we were standing in line at the grocery store, and he pointed to a 3 Musketeers bar and said, "That is the kind of candy I get when it's time to come home."

Aaron had never met his grandparents, but that day I knew for sure that he had somehow gotten to know them. My parents loved to fish, and 3 Musketeers was my father's favorite candy bar.

— **CANDY SPAHR**
East Berlin, Pennsylvania

My two-year-old granddaughter was spending the night with me. After sleeping a while, she suddenly sat straight up in bed and stared hard at something. I asked what she was looking at and she said, "Ronnie. He's over there." My 28-year-old son, Ron, had passed away when my granddaughter was six months old. "Ronnie" was his childhood nickname, yet it was never used past his elementary-school years. . . .

— **ANGELA BARBER**
Universal City, Texas

My grandson Jackson is three years old. When he was two, his grandpa—my husband, Todd—died suddenly and tragically from a motorcycle/semi accident. Jackson was, and I believe continues to be, very close with his grandfather. He has talked about memories he has with Grandpa, and talks to him often. Every day for the longest time he would take our wedding picture and have everyone kiss Grandpa, and then he would kiss it, too. He also likes a picture I have of Todd that sits on top of my bed frame. He grabbed it the other day and said, "I miss him, I miss him," and made a sad face.

His parents and I asked Jackson if he sees Todd, and he said yes. We asked him if Todd is in heaven, and he nodded yes. The other night he asked his mom why there are two lights next to Grandpa. We determined that the lights belong to Jackson's great-grandma and to one of Todd's dear friends who passed away a few months after Todd. Jackson continues to have conversations with his grandpa—and my daughter and I continue to keep Todd's loving presence alive in him.

— **BRENDA FLETCHER**
Faribault, New Mexico

In December 2007, my family lost my little brother, Mikey, to suicide. It was quite the experience to try to navigate, and the biggest learning opportunity of my life! I've felt him close to all of us many, many times before; however, in June 2008, we had an experience that shifted our believing into undeniable knowing.

My daughter, Jade, was 22 months old at the time. My grandfather had just passed, and my sister was visiting from Hawaii. My sister, my daughter, and I were lounging on my bed, getting ready to put my little one down for the night. All of a sudden we watched as Jade began to play off the side of the bed with someone unseen by our eyes but fully clear to her. We watched in amazement, as our hearts knew whom she was playing with.

Jade suddenly popped up and asked, "Where did Mikey go?" She looked around the bedroom until her gaze stopped at the end of my bed. "There he is," she said. She played a bit more, and my sister and I watched with tears streaming down our faces. Playtime ended, and I scooped up my bundle of light and love and took her to bed. She fell asleep almost instantly in peace.

I went back to the bedroom where my lovely sister still sat crying, almost in disbelief of what she had just seen and felt. We hugged and felt our love flow. We are forever grateful to have had each other there to experience this. It's so easy to deny these powerful experiences when you're alone—you seem able to talk yourself out of it actually happening. We are so blessed to have seen and felt the light of our dear brother. Since then we continue to hear from him and feel him in many different ways.

— **AMY LUTHER**
Heber City, Utah

My son, Steven, chose not to really talk until he was three, but he began with complete sentences. One morning he was playing nearby while I made his bed. I sensed he was engaged in a low-tone, but definite, dialogue with someone. I use "definite" because his sentences sounded posed as both statements and questions. After he spoke there would be a pause, while he apparently listened for a response, then he would continue.

I decided to interrupt him. "Stevie, who are you talking to?"

"The people where I came from."

"What are they wearing?

"They wear long white robes."

"Where are they? What are they saying?"

Impatiently, he said, "Oh, Mommy, you know. You were there, too."

With that, he went back to playing, refusing to speak further about it.

A few months later, immediately following the death of his great-grandmother, whom he had dubbed "Mom-Mom," he started having what sounded like two-way conversations. They occurred after he was tucked in bed and the lights had been turned out. After several evenings of hearing the ongoing murmurings, I slipped to his door to listen. I could not make out the words, but it was certainly a conversation. Finally, it stopped.

Softly calling his name so as to not startle him, I entered the darkened room and asked, "Stevie, who were you talking to?"

His happy reply was, "Mom-Mom."

"Where is she?"

"She comes every night and sits on my bed and talks to me." And with that, he rolled over and went to sleep.

Steven had no concept of death, nor did he know that Mom-Mom had passed over. Her nightly visits to sit on his bed and talk to him made perfect sense.

— **ELAINE L. WILSON**
New Cumberland, Pennsylvania

When my granddaughter was 20 months old, she reached through the railings of a second-story balcony, waved into thin air with a smile on her face, and said, "Boggie." This was the name of her great-great-grandmother. My daughter and I started crying; we both knew at that moment that angels were present. It was a great honor.

— **KAREN CRAVER-STANBURY**
Tyler, Texas

My 80-year-old father-in-law wanted to see his son and me have a baby more than anything. After my husband and I struggled for years to conceive and had several failed in-vitro attempts, we were delivered another blow when his father was diagnosed with cancer and ultimately lost the battle. Six months after my father-in-law's passing, we were blessed with a baby girl through adoption.

One night, my three-year-old daughter was sitting at my vanity while I was blow-drying her hair. She was looking into the mirror and singing, as she did every night when we did this. All of a sudden, she stopped singing and said, "Mommy, who is that old man?"

I whipped around expecting someone to be standing behind me, but nobody was there. I knew at that moment who she saw. I said, "That is your angel, baby. Poppy is here, and he is watching over you."

— **AMY SCHERRER***

When my niece was about three or four, my sister had moved into a new house. One day while speaking to their new neighbors, my niece mentioned that she had an imaginary friend name Lou who hung out with her all the time. The elderly couple was left speechless by that comment because their son, Lou, had lived in the house until his death two years before.

I know in my heart that this was not a coincidence, but Spirit alive and present in our lives every day. May we all be as open as a child!

— **IZZY LENIHAN***

My daughter's father (we had been divorced by this time) passed away when she was six. The day after the funeral, she asked from the backseat, "Why is Daddy surfing on the hood of the car?" I asked her what she could see, and she described it in clear terms. She said that he was waving good-bye, so I told her to answer him. She waved and shouted with vigor until he went away. And that was that—she moved on like it was nothing.

Then a couple of years later, we visited the grounds of a monastery close to our home. As we walked through the graveyard, my daughter got agitated and was letting me know not to walk in certain places. She fixed messy and crooked adornments to the graves (some were quite old), and as she fixed each one, she'd review it and pat the area and say, "There, there . . ." and move on. I watched her do this for about 20 minutes. It was busy work for a little girl, but finally she was good with her efforts and said we could go. She skipped away and that was all. I've recounted this story to her, and she has no recollection of it.

My daughter is 22 now. I've sent her links about Abraham [the wise collective consciousness facilitated by best-selling author Esther Hicks], and although I think she's looked at them, I also think she's a little afraid to. Last year we watched the movie *Cloud Atlas* together, and she wanted to talk all night because the concept was unsettling . . . like she knew something but couldn't identify it. She got really frustrated. I believe we still have these memories when we're older, but they zip past us and we just can't grab them.

— **SARAJANE TRIER**
Ontario, Canada

My mother-in-law, Frances, periodically babysat her great-niece, Felicia. They enjoyed being together, and then Frances passed away. The day after the death, Felicia's mother, Lisa, was giving her daughter a bath when they both heard the front door open and close. Lisa went out to see who it could be, but nobody was at the door or in the driveway. Upon returning to the bathroom, Felicia looked at her and said, "That was Aunt Frances. She said she has to go." Nobody had told her that Frances had died the day before.

There was one last time that Felicia saw Frances, in the summer of that same year. She had been swimming at her cousin's house, and it was time to go inside. She walked in with her grandmother (who was Frances's sister), and instead of going into the bathroom to change out of her bathing suit, Felicia insisted on going to the family room. When her grandma said, "No, not until you change," she yelled out, "Aunt Frances is sitting downstairs by herself! Can't you see her?" Stunned by those words, she let go of the child's hand, and Felicia proceeded down the stairs by herself. She returned upstairs a few moments later and said, "It's okay, I can get changed now."

Looking back, the adults who were there wished they had asked more questions about what she saw and what was said to her that day.

— **BETTY DIGIOVANNI**
Amherstburg, Ontario, Canada

My son, Daniel, attends a Catholic school. Once a week they have a class called "Continuous Praying," which is an initiative to teach children to get in touch with God and their own spirituality, and to learn the power of praying for others.

One day, my son, who was five years old (he's now six), came home and told me that he'd been laughing at Continuous Praying. I, of course, reprimanded him, telling him he had to concentrate and be respectful.

"I couldn't help it, Mom," he answered. "Tito Rigo told me a joke, and we were both laughing." Tito Rigo is the nickname he had for Rodrigo, my father, who had passed away one month before Daniel was conceived.

I had to find out more. "Really? Tito Rigo? Did you see him?"

"Well, yes, but not with my eyes—I saw him with my brain and my heart. I felt him over my head as always."

As always? "You see Tito Rigo often?"

"Not often."

"Well, what did he tell you?" I asked.

"He told me a joke, something about a banana. I didn't understand the joke, but I like him. He makes me laugh, and he wanted me to be happy."

I did know the joke—it was a silly one my father used to tell, with a game of words in Spanish. I was always sad that my father never got to meet any of his grandchildren. Now I know he didn't just meet them, but he even kept in touch with them.

I also have a story about my niece, Emma, who is a year younger than Daniel. One day, at age three or four, she came to my sister-in-law and said, "You know, I have two moms." Her other aunt used to babysit her every day, so my sister-in-law answered, "Yes, Emma, Nana is sometimes like your mom when I am away."

"No, Momma, not Nana. Mary. The lady in the long dress told me her name was Mary and that she was my mom, too."

My sister-in-law was amazed. She opened her laptop, looked for images of the Virgin Mary, and asked Emma if this was the lady. My niece said, "Looks like her, with the dress pink and light blue, and the crown. But she had more light." And then she changed the subject.

— **PAULA ACUÑA**
San José, Costa Rica

When my son was an infant (he's now nine), I took him to California from our home in New York to meet his great-great-aunt. We went to the hospital to visit her, and my son sat on her lap. Two days after we returned home, I received word from my cousins that Aunt Joyce had passed.

A few years later, my son and I were playing "badoon," as he so often referred to his favorite balloon game. The game consisted of bopping the balloon back and forth, trying to keep it in the air so as not to have it touch the floor. I was sitting on a rocking chair waiting my turn, with my feet resting on a footstool. The footstool was my great-aunt's—my cousin had given it to me, having me stuff it in my suitcase to bring it back home with us.

As the balloon was floating back and forth between us, my son lit up and said, "Aunt Joyce." Surprised, I asked him what he had said. With a beaming smile, he repeated, "Aunt Joyce."

My husband was sitting nearby, gazing over work plans at the dining-room table, and I checked to see if he just heard what our son had said. When he said yes, I turned back to our son and asked, "What about Aunt Joyce?" He smiled and shrugged while returning the balloon to me.

I then recalled a memory, which I shared with my husband: a couple of months before, I'd had a dream with Aunt Joyce in it, and she'd told me that she'd be seeing us at the holidays. I then smiled as I realized it was almost Thanksgiving. I said a gratitude prayer, then telephoned my aunt's daughter after the "badoon" game was finished.

When I talk with my son now about his dreams and plans for his future, he tells me, "I'm not sure, Mom, other than I want to be happy."

— **MARIA JACKSON**
Phoenix, New York

When my 24-year-old daughter, Lauren, was a child, she had an imaginary friend whose name was also Lauren; my daughter called her "the other Lauren." She spoke to Lauren all the time as if she could see her. My pediatrician and friends said it was totally normal and to leave it alone.

One day we sat down to lunch and I asked my daughter why I couldn't see "the other Lauren." She said because she was dead, and that she was around three years old.

We moved when Lauren was seven, and we never heard about "the other Lauren" again. I once asked my daughter about it, and she said that she lives at the old house.

— **DONNA DALEY***

When my son, Jack, was two or three he would cry that he missed his poppy. My father died years before he was born. At the time I wasn't very spiritual and told him, "He died before you were born, honey." He insisted that Poppy had taught him to run and ride a bike, and spoke of a dog they had. (He was riding his bike without training wheels by the time he was three, so maybe my dad did gave him some private lessons before he came here . . .)

— **KATIE FIRMSTONE**
Honesdale, Pennsylvania

My son had a very special (imaginary) friend named Jim Howard, who was a part of our lives until my son reached the age of six. We made a move out of state, and my son told me Jim Howard did not want to come with us. That was the end of Jim Howard.

— **NANCI STONE**
Las Vegas, Nevada

My daughter, Felicia, had two "make believe" friends, Johnny and Lisa, who sat at the table with us and went everywhere we went—and heaven forbid that anyone try to sit on the reserved chairs. She'd talk to and play with them just as though they were little humans sitting next to her. I always believed they were her two guardian angels.

— **RACHAEL GONZALEZ**
Las Cruces, New Mexico

I once saw my friend's four-year-old son coming up the short staircase between levels of the restaurant where we were dining, with one arm akimbo at his side and the opposite hand holding the rail. I asked, "Why is he walking like that?" and his mother replied, "Oh, he's always doing things like that. His imaginary friend is an old man."

— **DANA H.***

When my daughter was a little one, she had an imaginary friend named Sarah, whom I would find her talking to a great deal. She would be sitting at the table, or what have you, and the family welcomed Sarah.

At the time I thought my daughter was lonely because I couldn't have any more children, and then over time Sarah wasn't there.

My daughter is now 13, and she does remember Sarah and what she looked like. I wonder now, was Sarah a spirit in our old house or was she a relative from the past guiding my daughter? There is so much we don't understand about our children's imaginary friends.

— **KAREN SOUTHWELL**
Maitland, Australia

My mom and dad were both free spirits, and they raised seven children together. Daddy passed away from a heart attack 11 years ago. Mommy was one of a kind—the most beautiful, amazing person I've ever known—and just recently died from cancer at the age of 59. A week after her passing, my two-year-old niece, Miley, who is the youngest child in our family, spoke of a visitation from her grandma.

Everyone was going to sleep when she shouted "Grandma Julie!" Her parents looked confused as she pointed outside. She said, "Grandma Julie outside. I see her." When her dad woke up at 4 A.M. to go to work, Miley was up and out of bed, sitting against the sliding-glass door where she had pointed the night before.

Weeks went by and Miley kept saying that she wanted to see Grandma Julie outside again, so her mom began to ask questions. My niece said that she'd seen Grandma outside wearing a "lavender princess dress," which is interesting because a few weeks before Mommy died, a friend had given her a light purple princess dress, but she was too sick to ever wear it.

Miley then told her mom to put on "the princess movie." When the movie started, she pointed to the clouds and said, "See, Grandma Julie like that." She said that Grandma was smiling and demonstrated how. Then her mom was overcome with chills when she said, "Grandpa there, too."

Miley's parents did not have very many pictures of my dad and had never really spoken of him to her. Her mom showed her a picture of him, and she said, "Yes, Grandpa Lee."

"Did they say anything to you, Miley?"

She said, "Yes, Grandma said she had to go bye-bye in the sky." She spoke of the stars and pointed up. Her mom asked if Grandpa Lee had said anything to her, and she said, "Yes, Grandpa told Grandma that he wanted to meet me." Then she said that she tried to give him kisses, but he was too far in the sky and she couldn't reach him.

Thank you, Miley, for letting us know that our parents are together and that they are happy. Heaven is for real, and I know that I will see them both again when my time comes.

I love you, Mommy and Daddy.

— **CHRISTIE CLIETT**
Maui, Hawaii

My grandson, Kuvay, who is six, never met my father because he passed away five years before Kuvay was born. Kuvay is keen to go fishing and is very good at it—he says that my dad taught him his fishing skills.

— **HAZEL REDDY**
Empangeni, South Africa

When my mom died at the age of ninety, my granddaughter, Sophie, was two and a half. As we adults sat around for several days doing all the stuff you have to do when someone passes, I made the comment, "I wish Mom was here—she'd just love all of this."

Sophie pointed down the hall and said, "But she is here. She is right down the hall."

I know that my mom was there, and my grand-daughter saw her. We adults couldn't see her because we were too far removed from Spirit, but Sophie and Mom were right there!

— **BOB BOLLMANN**
Hemet, California

My two-year-old son once made a comment as he sat at the edge of the bed: "Grandma says that you have a beautiful home." Since Grandma had passed in the early '60s, I asked him how he knew this. He answered, "She is right here next to me."

— **ANGIE CABANAS-MARTILOTTO**
Weston, Florida

My young cousin died last year of cancer, leaving behind a little girl who had just turned two. Within three hours of her passing, her daughter (who was being minded by a neighbor) was sitting at the window and waved at the sky. Then she turned to the neighbor and said, "Mummie's gone bye-bye."

— **DONNA ROMEO**
Thornlands, Queensland, Australia

My grandma had recently passed away, and I took my two-and-a-half-year-old to her grave. My daughter was chattering away next to me, and I thought she was just playing. When I asked who she was talking to while she was playing, and she said, "Grandma." I asked what she looked like, and my daughter said, "Her was pretty and had hair." My grandma had lung cancer, and the chemo had made her hair fall out before she died.

I asked what she was wearing, and my daughter said, "White" and that she "kissed and hugged me." While I was amazed, my daughter acted as if it were no big deal, and so I wonder how often our past friends and family visit our small ones.

— **BROOKE JENKINS**
Riverton, Utah

When my granddaughter was three, she lost her paternal grandfather. One night she came to visit, and out of the blue said, "Grandpa Peter comes to my room every night and tucks me in and tells me he loves me." I asked if he was by himself, and she replied, "Sometimes he has friends with him."

— **MARILYN LAGO**
Boca Raton, Florida

I had a very old and wise spiritual teacher named Bawa Muhaiyaddeen. He married my husband and me and named our daughter, Sulaiha. When Sulaiha was ten months old, her daddy was diagnosed with lung cancer. They were very close, and he told her he had to "go away and could not come back," and it was not her fault. Bawa passed when she was two, and when her dad spoke to her about his own impending death, she said, "Then you will be with Bawa."

Of course we never knew exactly when he was going to pass—it turned out that her daddy passed when Sulaiha was two years and ten months old. On the morning of that fated day, she woke up and said, "Bawa came to see Daddy last night!"

I was humored and asked, "What did Bawa say?"

She replied, "Salaam [peace] and have a cup of tea." This was something Bawa always did to a newcomer to his ashram.

That night my husband passed peacefully. It was as if our daughter had seen this coming of the angel of death, who will appear as a loved one, spiritual teacher, or someone like Jesus, so that you are not afraid.

Sulaiha never cried. She was my biggest comfort and did not grieve until she was six years old. This was triggered when her first-grade teacher asked the class to write about their family, how many people were in it, who named them, and when they were born. The grief was something that lasted a whole year.

My daughter is now 30—to this day, she is still very intuitive, and her ability to see things on an unseen level and depth endures. She met a wonderful man who also shares her sensibilities. I am so blessed.

— **LINDA M. SCHWARTZ**
Merion Station, Pennsylvania

The greatest gift any of us have been given is the gift of our imagination. Everything that now exists in the physical universe was once imagined. I urge you to allow not only your child's imagination to run rampantly, but your own as well. Here is what one of the smartest humans who ever lived on this planet, Dr. Albert Einstein, had to say on this topic: "If you want your children to be intelligent, read them fairy tales. If you want them to be more intelligent, read them more fairy tales."

A child's fanciful excursions into the world of invisible friends and sightings of apparitions can very well be like reading them fairy tales. Rather than being the least bit judgmental, allow your child's imagination to soar in whatever direction they may wish to express it. And remember at all times that just because you fail to see what a child is pointing to, it does not mean that what they see is unreal. As Albert Einstein indicated is his famous observation, a child using their imagination without criticism is one of the surest ways they can become even "more intelligent." They may also have something to teach you about using your own imagination more creatively. Maybe it's time for *you* to read more fairy tales.

8

ANGEL STORIES

∽ I believe in angels. I have had personal experiences in which I have been escorted out of extreme danger by beings who took my hand and led me to safety. And when my wife, Marcelene, was giving birth to her first child, she was assisted in her labor by a nurse whom she could describe in great detail—but it turns out that no one who worked in the delivery room at the hospital had ever seen this nurse.

I have been to the site in Lourdes where St. Bernadette had 18 visitations from an apparition of the Virgin Mary. I climbed the mountain in Medjugorje where six children saw the same vision of the Blessed Mother, and are still seeing her regularly almost 35 years later.

The spiritual literature is replete with references to the presence of guardian angels who are available to assist us on this temporary journey here on Earth. In the ancient sacred text called the Talmud, there are these words written back in the 8th century: "Every blade of grass has its angel that bends over it and whispers, 'Grow, grow.'" Surely if the grass in the field has angelic guidance available to fulfill its purpose, there ought to be celestial counsel at one's disposal for all of us humans as well.

In the 13th century, the brilliant philosopher St. Thomas Aquinas offered us this penetrating understanding about the presence of angels among us: "We are like children, who stand in need of masters to enlighten us and direct us; God has provided for this by appointing his angels to be our teachers and guides." The children's reports in this chapter reflect the truth of what this eminent scholar writes about the presence of God's emissaries among us, containing many references to the sightings of angels and delivered with absolute certainty and wisdom. Perhaps because young children have not been conditioned to believe otherwise, they are able to see and feel this guidance, whereas others who are shaped by fear and doubt remain in a state of blissful ignorance.

My all-time favorite poet, William Blake, used the imagery of angels throughout his vast collected works. Here is what he wrote concerning the presence of angels in the lives of children: "The angel that presided o'er my birth / Said 'Little creature, form'd of joy and mirth, / Go, love without the help of anything on Earth.'" These sweet loving beings we have come to call angels are certainly not of this material world. Blake asks us to listen to these

My youngest daughter used to tell me that at night she returned to heaven and an angel would come and get her. They would fly in the sky, through space, and arrive at heaven. While there she saw my father, who had passed ten years before—he had a house and was growing yellow roses for my mother. (My mother is still alive at age 84.) Then, she said, "When the bells start to ring, you have to leave."

Today my daughter is a young adult and doesn't remember this. At the time she told me, I thought how amazing this was! And I still do.

— **SANDRA RAMAGE McGLEISH**
Fort Myers, Florida

My son, Harrison, is almost seven years old and has been interested in talking about God and angels since he was young. I pray with him nightly, and he often reminds me if I forget, even at dinner. He has a certain curiosity about him—he has asked me all sorts of questions about heaven, God, angels, and how many years we will live. He thinks we all should live to at least 100.

When Harrison was five, he and I were having breakfast one morning and talking about superheroes, Ninja Turtles, and the like. All of a sudden, he asked me if we did this very often. I said, "What, breakfast? Yes, we do this every morning." He pointed up and down and said, "Go from heaven to earth?" I asked him what he thought, and he said that he thinks we do. Then he went back to talking superheroes.

Around this time, my son was having horrible night terrors, and I recommended that he ask Archangel Michael to help him. When I asked how it went, he told me Michael was like an angel superhero because he wears a white robe with a yellow belt and had a sword to fight the "bad guys." As far as I know, he hadn't even been shown a picture of Michael specifically . . . and Harrison said that he'd met him.

— **SHAWN LAYMAN**
Indianapolis, Indiana

My first son, Trevor, began to talk quite early. He was around 18 months old when I was feeding him his little toddler meal in the high chair one night, and he said, "Nonni," and pointed to the sky. I had to ask him about it several times, and then got a picture off the wall of my husband's Italian grandmother. My son pointed to the picture and said, "Nonni," with a huge grin on his face.

Nonni had passed away before Trevor was born, and we really didn't talk about her that much. I asked him, "Where is Nonni?" and he pointed up to the sky.

"What does Nonni do?"

"She talks."

"Talks? What does she say?"

He took his finger up to his mouth and went, "Shh . . ." Then he giggled.

My second son, Gavin, began talking to Nonni when *he* was about 18 months old—this time I wasn't as surprised. He also talked to Papa, Nonni's husband, so I asked him about them. "They are my angel friends."

"What do they do?" I asked.

"They play games with me . . . Papa has the baby," he said. "Papa has all the babies." There is no way that my son would have known that my husband and I had lost two pregnancies in miscarriage. My husband's cousin and his wife had also recently lost a baby to preterm labor that was five months along. How amazing to hear from this little child that "Papa has all the babies"!

When I asked Gavin what Papa did with the babies, he replied, "He rocks them like this," and made his hands like a cradle and pretended to rock a baby. He talked about Nonni and Papa for a few weeks and then one day he said to me, "Nonni is going back to heaven now. She is going down the blue tunnel." And that was that.

Gavin still talks to his guardian angels at the age of eight. Just recently he told me that he'd received information that the angels were excited about sending babies from heaven to people we knew. That week, we found out three of our friends were newly expecting babies and hadn't told anyone else yet.

— **BONNIE WALLACE**
Auburn, Massachusetts

I have two sons, ages 12 and 16. One night when my older son was about eight, a friend of his slept over, and the three boys decided to camp out on the living-room floor. The next day my youngest, who was five at the time, told me that he'd been awakened in the middle of the night by a very bright light. When he looked up, he'd seen a lady floating and glowing above the TV, and the light was blinding. He woke the other boys up, who saw the same thing. I verified this angel sighting with the older boys at different times, and I am convinced that they did see an angel. They all said that the lady stared at them for a while and then disappeared. At that time, I had never had a conversation about angels with my children.

On another occasion, when my younger son was about nine, my husband had traveled out of the country.

The night he left, I prayed to God, and prayed that Archangel Michael would protect us. The very next morning, my son and I were in the kitchen area when all of a sudden I saw him do a double take, looking at the sofa in the living room. He said, "Mom, did you see that man? He was sitting with his right arm resting on the arm of the sofa—he was very transparent, and I could only see him from the chest up. He was staring at us in the kitchen, and the moment our eyes met, he disappeared."

Lo and behold, when we went over to the sofa, we indeed saw what looked like an indentation of where an arm or an elbow had been resting. I believe my son saw Archangel Michael. I also believe that the angel had shown itself to my son because when I'd prayed to him, I'd said, "Please let me know you are protecting us. I don't want to see you, though, as I am easily scared." So Michael had shown himself to my son, who was more open.

Neither of my boys have had any more angel sightings since then.

— **TARELA SHITTU**
Edmonton, Alberta, Canada

When my daughter, Sky, was about 4 years old (she's now 21), something happened that I remember as vividly as if it were yesterday. As we were beginning our day, she gave me a detailed description of an encounter she'd had with an angel. She went on about how this diminutive angel was dressed, all in white; how she sat on the dresser, which was approximately eye level with Sky as she sat up in bed; and how she told Sky that she would be by her side, because she was going to be needed.

The angel also said that her mommy had gone through four "not births" before Sky was born. The angel told Sky that she was very much wanted by her father and me, and also by the spirit realm. Sky actually used those two words. She said, "Yes, Mommy, I'm sure, the angel said the spirit realm."

I was rendered speechless—I'd in fact had four miscarriages and nearly miscarried Sky. I later found out that I'd been born with an abnormality called a "tipped uterus." You can't imagine what her father and I had gone through to get to term with Sky, who was born a month early but weighed a healthy six pounds, two ounces.

My daughter distinctly informed me that the little angel told her that she was meant for a higher purpose, that prior to her birth she was made of pure light, and that she chose her parents and the difficulties she'd have to face as she grew older.) As time went on, she'd ask me, "Mommy, what problems will I go through?"

I didn't have any idea, although I did know that alcoholism ran in my family on both sides. So I am embarrassed to say this, but by the time she was 12, Sky did need her angel because of me. I became addicted to drugs so terribly that if it weren't for Sky's wonderful father, she surely would have been placed with other family members. My addiction led to prison time, but I'm happy to say that I have been ten years clean this November.

Sky has more than thrived: She is entering her senior year at college, and has never tried drugs nor touched a drink or cigarettes. She had more than one visit from the tiny angel but says now that she doesn't have any recollection of what occurred when she was four. My daughter is very matter-of-fact, and I believe with all my heart that she *does* remember but won't or can't talk about it. For some reason, she doesn't believe whatsoever in the spiritual world.

I know that this soul, my Sky, was meant to be here, for what I do not know, other than to bring her father and me joy every day. She's bright and articulate, and we are so proud of her.

— **DENISE GOSDEN**
West Palm Beach, Florida

When my children were in early adolescence (around the age of ten), I allowed them to search for their own spiritual growth. If they had questions, I'd help them find answers to allow them to form their own opinions and beliefs. Prior to that age, though, I said nothing because I wanted their beautiful minds open to possibilities, not boundaries.

When my youngest was five (prior to going to school), she and I were swimming in our apartment pool. She was terrified of water—even baths—from the time she was born, but I wanted her to learn how to swim for her own protection. That day she was particularly calm, and I was so grateful because she was open to listening to my directions. I taught her how to find her buoyancy and was showing her how to kick when she stated, "Mommy, I talked to the angel Gabriel last night." I was shocked because the idea of angels and their existence had not been spoken about by me in such a detailed way.

Keeping my voice neutral, I asked, "Really? What did Gabriel look like?"

"*She* looked like a *star.*"

I nodded my head, then asked, "What did you two talk about?"

"She taught me about math."

"Wow, that sounds like fun."

"It was fun. Oh, and she said not to be afraid of water."

"I agree."

Turns out, according to legend, Gabriel is the only angel who will appear as male or female to a person, and also rules over water and emotions.

My daughter is 26 years old now. She swims like a fish and is an astrophysics major at Arizona State University, having been fascinated by the cosmos since that time. She just finished her first internship at an observatory in North Carolina, and is working on her first scientific paper based on a star known as VX Her. My scientist claims atheism now. I smile when she says that because she still remembers the "dream" of Gabriel to this day.

— **ERIN SIKES-BRUCE***

From the time my son, Jacob, could talk (he's now almost 15), he had these "friends" he called "Baygas." There was Fat Bayga, Skinny Bayga, Dark Bayga, Light Bayga . . . the list goes on and on. One day I asked him who these Baygas were, and with a smile he said that they were angels and he helped them protect us!

— **PHYLLIS KEENE WOODALL**
Marietta, Georgia

My youngest daughter used to have conversations with angels every night. One night when she was just two and a half, she asked me to tell them not to have so many in her room because she was tired and wanted to sleep some more. I told her to ask the angels not to stay that night, and we did it together. The next morning when I asked her how she slept, she told me that only "Michael" had stayed at the foot of her bed to help her sleep more peacefully. I got chills, knowing who Michael was. When she noticed my reaction, she said, "Yep, Mommy, he's my favorite, too!" I'd never told her angel names—I always let her tell me.

As an added note, my Northern California–born baby began her talking days speaking in a *very* strong Boston accent! No one in our family had ever been to Boston, and she always told me it was "from before."

— **TERI BAKER SCHAFFER**
Pleasanton, California

I have two babies. My eldest, who is three years old, says a lot of things that sometimes sound weird but are quite intuitive. For example, I have an old photo album with pictures of my parents and family, along with my husband's family. He loves to see the album and one day said, "Momma, those are my angel grandparents who live in Colombia."

I was surprised because my mom died 11 years ago, but my dad passed just 7 months ago and I never told my son about that. Anyway, I said, "Yes, honey, they are angels." Last week he suddenly said, "Momma, my angel grandparents said that they take care of me but aren't taking care of you anymore . . ."

Every time he says something like this, it leaves me without words.

— **CARMEN LILIANA MEJIA**
Hollywood, Florida

When my granddaughter was about three, we had an interesting encounter with a deer that walked right up to us as I was putting her in the backseat of my car. I told her not to be frightened and asked the deer to please step back, and he did. As we were pulling away, I heard my granddaughter talking to someone. I asked who it was, and she said her angels. She told me that they were sorry I couldn't see them, but to tell me that someday I will. I of course believed her! She is a gift and a blessing to our earth.

— **MARY KAY BRANT**
Eugene, Oregon

When my older son was about 5 (he's now 23), I was reading to him from a book about angels. As I tucked him in, I asked, "Have you ever seen an angel?" He looked at me like "Duh!" and said with absolute clarity and confidence: "Of course! I see them all the time. They come visit me in the middle of the night when you're not here."

— **ERIC McPHERSON***

I had an experience with our daughter, Amber, who is now 37, that I will always remember. When she was about two, she told my husband, Gary, and myself that she was an angel from angel land and that she came from a cloud "kind of like that one" (she looked into the sky and pointed to a cloud hovering above). She told us that she wore a purple dress, and her other little angel friends had pretty dresses, too, like pink and blue. Gary and I smiled and thought, *How cute,* and left it at that.

Many years later, this event came back into my mind, and I had the realization that we'd never talked about angels to Amber, yet she talked about them with us. I wish that back then I would have just sat with her and asked more questions, but it was not meant to be. That's okay, for I will always have the wonderful remembrance of that experience.

— **CAROLE CLARK**
Dunedin, Florida

I was on the way to drop my four-year-old, Marc, off at day care. We drove for a while and then he said, "Mommy, you are so beautiful." I thanked him, and he said, "Yes, you are so beautiful with all of the angels around your head!" When I told him that was very sweet, he insisted, "Mommy, they are all around your head," and then looked down to keep playing with his toy like it was no big deal.

There was such a feeling of love in that car I cannot begin to describe. I will always remember that special morning!

— **DR. DEBBIE BAKER**
Hampden, Maine

My daughter Cassidy was my little surprise. But the funny thing is that I dreamed of her months before I got pregnant—I dreamed that I would have another little girl, even though I hadn't planned on having more children. When she was a baby of about 10 to 15 months old, we enjoyed playing in the backyard, and my daughter would giggle up a storm and look up to the sky. I always wondered what she was imagining. Then one day she pointed toward the roof of our house, happy as could be, and said, "Angel baby" through her giggles. She kept doing this for several months almost every time we were outside, and then it just stopped as she got older.

Today Cassidy is 16 and has no recollection of those events. Yet I believe that she did see something through the innocence of her soul!

— **ROBIN BLANCHARD***

I have identical twin daughters who are now 21. When they were between the ages of two and three, I was getting ready for work. The girls were playing, and talking with me while they watched me apply my makeup. One of them said, "Mommy, now that we eat real food, the angels don't come as often." I asked what she meant, and the other one replied, "Now that we don't drink milk out of bottles and we eat food, they don't come as often."

This really blew me away because at that young of an age I knew they had no concept of what they had just said, and were merely speaking the truth!

— **DEBRA RIEHL**
Toms River, New Jersey

Like a lot of parents, I was able to enjoy and wonder at my son's memories from his recent connection to the spirit world. I found that the younger Shane was, the stronger his connection; as the years went by, I was saddened to watch that fade. I specifically remember the day when I asked him (for the millionth time, in order for him to remember) to tell me about a previous life experience. As he started to tell me his stories, I was crushed to see how the words and memories were crumbling even as he spoke. I realize now that this was the moment he started to doubt himself and his memories. My son was four years old when I witnessed this loss of his spirit connection.

Shane is a 17-year-old high-school senior now, but one of my favorite memories of him was when he was 3. I was always a single mom, and at the time I was working long hours in California's Silicon Valley, fortunate enough to work for a very successful high-tech company that gave me stock options. It was a proud day when I was able to buy a small home and then get my son the race-car bed he wanted, as I had promised him that I would provide those things for him one day.

One of the first few times I took my son to see our new home, he had a very profound experience as we were pulling into our driveway. Before I could pull all the way in, Shane started carrying on and screaming at the top of his lungs (which was uncharacteristic of him), while pointing to the roof of our home, "Oh, *look*, Mommy! Look! They are sooo beautiful! See them, Mommy? See them?"

I stopped the car, then turned around to him and asked very sternly what he was talking about. I have to admit I was worried at this point. He smiled, giggled, and replied, "Oh, Mommy, they are dancing! Their wings are big and gold . . . they are dancing!"

I'll never forget that moment because I got instant goose bumps and began to smile and cry at the same time. I felt so blessed that these beautiful angels were on the roof of our home, dancing and celebrating. But what warmed my heart more than anything is that my sweet son was so connected to it all that he could actually see these beautiful angels! I'll never forget his joy and happiness as he described to me what was taking place.

— **KIKI MAVRIDIS**
Kansas City, Missouri

Open yourself up to the possibility of attracting angelic guidance. This is accomplished by aligning yourself with the Divine realm. Lao-tzu, the philosopher and poet of ancient China, says that if we wish to become Divine beings ourselves, then we must restore our Divine qualities through virtue and service.

I believe that young children are examples of beings who see and feel the presence of angels because they live virtuous, nonjudgmental lives. It seems that this angelic communication that little boys and girls report so frequently comes to them without their seeking. And this is in large part because angels recognize their own Divine qualities in those who have yet to be victimized by their own egos.

As Lao-tzu tells us, taming our egoistic inclinations is the only way to gain the attention of the immortals who instruct us in what is necessary to reach the Divine realm. Our children seem to have this awareness, so I urge you to emulate their virtuous qualities and note the angelic presences that will begin to show up for *you*.

AFTERWORD

I'd like to return to William Wordsworth's "Ode: Intimations of Immortality from Recollections of Early Childhood," which I referenced earlier in the book. Two lines from this poem stand out for me, and their meaning became even more unclouded as I read and chronicled so many stories from parents and family members from all over the world.

I discussed the first, "Our birth is but a sleep and a forgetting," in the Introduction. The other line of Wordsworth's poem, which has captivated me for my entire lifetime, is, "Heaven lies about us in our infancy!" This speaks to me in a very big way. *Heaven* is the word that describes perfect bliss, infinite peace, and above all, Divine love: A kind of love that never varies and never changes. A state of being in which there are no opposites; it is pure oneness.

Everything is pure love. In fact, in the New Testament, Jesus tells us, "The light of the body is the eye: if therefore thine eye be single, thy whole body shall be full of light" (Matthew 6:22). This means that when we use our human eyes to see only oneness, rather than all of the dualities that make for conflict, sadness, and pain, we are experiencing what heaven is really like. And, as Wordsworth reminds us so poignantly, heaven lies about us in our infancy. This is what we emanated from, this is our original nature, and this is precisely what our recent arrivals from the oneness have to offer us, a sweet taste of heaven that lies about all of us whose "eye be single."

Dee and I hope that the words from young children we have brought you in this book will help you recapture your own sense of innocence and feeling of being loved by Spirit.

— I AM,

Wayne W. Dyer

ABOUT THE AUTHORS

Affectionately called the "father of motivation" by his fans, **Dr. Wayne W. Dyer** was an internationally renowned author, speaker, and pioneer in the field of self-development. Over the four decades of his career, he wrote more than 40 books (21 of which became *New York Times* bestsellers), created numerous audio programs and videos, and appeared on thousands of television and radio shows. His books *Manifest Your Destiny, Wisdom of the Ages, There's a Spiritual Solution to Every Problem,* and the *New York Times* bestsellers *10 Secrets for Success and Inner Peace, The Power of Intention, Inspiration, Change Your Thoughts—Change Your Life, Excuses Begone!, Wishes Fulfilled,* and *I Can See Clearly Now* were all featured as National Public Television specials.

Wayne held a doctorate in educational counseling from Wayne State University, had been an associate professor at St. John's University in New York, and honored a lifetime commitment to learning and finding the Higher Self. In 2015, he left his body, returning to Infinite Source to embark on his next adventure.

Website: www.DrWayneDyer.com

Dee Garnes currently resides in Maui with her husband and two children. She has worked in the healing-arts field as a massage therapist for over 13 years, and was an assistant to Dr. Wayne Dyer. In her free time, when she is not chasing her two-year-old son around or caring for her infant daughter, she enjoys long-distance swims in the ocean, paddleboarding, and hiking. Her longest hike to date spanned 50 days across the 500-mile Colorado Trail.

Hay House Titles of Related Interest

YOU CAN HEAL YOUR LIFE, the movie, starring Louise Hay & Friends
(available as a 1-DVD program and an expanded 2-DVD set)
Watch the trailer at: www.LouiseHayMovie.com

THE SHIFT, the movie,
starring Dr. Wayne W. Dyer
(available as a 1-DVD program and an expanded 2-DVD set)
Watch the trailer at: www.DyerMovie.com

ADVENTURES OF THE SOUL: Journeys Through the Physical
and Spiritual Dimensions, by James Van Praagh

BEYOND PAST LIVES: What Parallel Realities Can Teach Us about
Relationships, Healing, and Transformation, by Mira Kelley

THE INDIGO CHILDREN: The New Kids Have
Arrived, by Lee Carroll and Jan Tober

MIRRORS OF TIME: Using Regression for Physical, Emotional,
and Spiritual Healing, by Brian L. Weiss, M.D.

SAVED BY AN ANGEL: True Accounts of People Who
Have Had Extraordinary Experiences with Angels . . .
and How YOU Can, Too! by Doreen Virtue

All of the above are available at your local bookstore,
or may be ordered by contacting Hay House (see next page).

We hope you enjoyed this Hay House book. If you'd like to receive our online catalog featuring additional information on Hay House books and products, or if you'd like to find out more about the Hay Foundation, please contact:

Hay House, Inc., P.O. Box 5100, Carlsbad, CA 92018-5100
(760) 431-7695 or (800) 654-5126
(760) 431-6948 (fax) or (800) 650-5115 (fax)
www.hayhouse.com® • www.hayfoundation.org

Published and distributed in Australia by:
Hay House Australia Pty. Ltd., 18/36 Ralph St., Alexandria NSW 2015
Phone: 612-9669-4299 • *Fax:* 612-9669-4144 • www.hayhouse.com.au

Published and distributed in the United Kingdom by:
Hay House UK, Ltd., Astley House, 33 Notting Hill Gate, London W11 3JQ
• *Phone:* 44-20-3675-2450 *Fax:* 44-20-3675-2451 • www.hayhouse.co.uk

Published and distributed in the Republic of South Africa by:
Hay House SA (Pty), Ltd., P.O. Box 990, Witkoppen 2068
info@hayhouse.co.za • www.hayhouse.co.za

Published in India by:
Hay House Publishers India, Muskaan Complex, Plot No. 3, B-2,
Vasant Kunj, New Delhi 110 070 *Phone:* 91-11-4176-1620
Fax: 91-11-4176-1630 • www.hayhouse.co.in

Distributed in Canada by:
Raincoast Books, 2440 Viking Way, Richmond, B.C. V6V 1N2
Phone: 1-800-663-5714 • *Fax:* 1-800-565-3770 • www.raincoast.com

Take Your Soul on a Vacation

Visit www.HealYourLife.com® to regroup, recharge, and reconnect with your own magnificence. Featuring blogs, mind-body-spirit news, and life-changing wisdom from Louise Hay and friends.

Visit www.HealYourLife.com today!

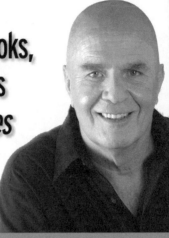

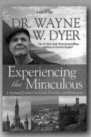